How to Manage your [illegible] Open Learning Course

Palgrave Study Guides

Authoring a PhD
Career Skills
e-Learning Skills
Effective Communication for Arts and Humanities Students
Effective Communication for Science and Technology
The Foundations of Research
The Good Supervisor
How to Manage your Arts Humanities and Social Science Degree
How to Manage your Distance and Open Learning Course
How to Manage your Postgraduate Course
How to Manage your Science and Technology Degree
How to Study Foreign Languages
How to Write Better Essays
Making Sense of Statistics
The Mature Student's Guide to Writing
The Postgraduate Research Handbook
Presentation Skills for Students
The Principles of Writing in Psychology
Professional Writing
Research Using IT
Skills for Success
The Student's Guide to Writing
The Study Skills Handbook (2nd edn)
Study Skills for Speakers of English as a Second Language
Studying the Built Environment
Studying Economics
Studying History (2nd edn)
Studying Mathematics and its Applications
Studying Modern Drama (2nd edn)
Studying Physics
Studying Psychology
Teaching Study Skills and Supporting Learning
Work Placements – a Survival Guide for Students
Writing for Engineers

Palgrave Study Guides Literature
General Editors:John Peck and Martin Coyle

How to Begin Studying English Literature (3rd edn)
How to Study a Jane Austen Novel (2nd edn)
How to Study a Charles Dickens Novel
How to Study Chaucer (2nd edn)
How to Study an E.M.Forster Novel
How to Study James Joyce
How to Study Linguistics (2nd edn)
How to Study Modern Poetry
How to Study a Novel (2nd edn)
How to Study a Poet (2nd edn)
How to Study a Renaissance Play
How to Study Romantic Poetry (2nd edn)
How to Study a Shakespeare Play (2nd edn)
How to Study Television
Practical Criticism

How to Manage your Distance and Open Learning Course

Lucinda Becker

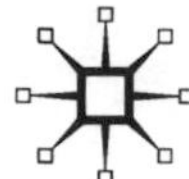

First published 2004 by
PALGRAVE MACMILLAN
Houndmills, Basingstoke, Hampshire RG21 6XS and
175 Fifth Avenue, New York, N.Y. 10010
Companies and representatives throughout the world

PALGRAVE MACMILLAN is the global academic imprint of the Palgrave Macmillan division of St. Martin's Press, LLC and of Palgrave Macmillan Ltd. Macmillan® is a registered trademark in the United States, United Kingdom and other countries. Palgrave is a registered trademark in the European Union and other countries.

ISBN 1–4039–2152–0

This book is printed on paper suitable for recycling and made from fully managed and sustained forest sources.

A catalogue record for this book is available from the British Library.

10 9 8 7 6 5 4 3 2 1
13 12 11 10 09 08 07 06 05 04

Printed and bound in Great Britain by
Creative Print & Design (Wales), Ebbw Vale

Contents

Acknowledgements

I would like to thank my family, Phil, Anastasia and Felicity, for their prolonged patience during this project. I am also grateful to Paul McColm for his valuable advice and support.

1 Introduction

A distance or open learning course requires much more than simply mastering your subject. It also asks that you develop a variety of study and management skills, such as time management, varying learning techniques and the ability to structure and present your thoughts in a logical and authoritative way. This might seem like a lot to expect of you as you face the prospect of a new course, but these skills, once acquired, will be of benefit to you throughout your course and beyond. It is often the management skills you learn on a course that stay with you longer than any formal part of the learning process. The good news is that once you have begun to master these challenges, you will find your course easier, more manageable and ultimately more satisfying. This book is designed to help you to identify your learning and management needs, and then to understand and develop them in the light of the demands of your course. It does not overlook the fact that you might need help with basic study techniques, such as tackling a reading list or producing an effective essay, but it will take you further than this, exploring each aspect of a distance and open learning course and guiding you through every learning situation as you progress.

Because the scope of this book is so wide, it has been designed to be as accessible as possible. Whilst you may find it useful to read through the whole book in the first stages of your course, as your study situation develops, you might need to refer to just one or two sections to remind yourself of the principles involved in managing certain aspects of your course. For this reason there is a 'troubleshooting guide' at the opening of each chapter, aimed to help you to identify the relevant section for your needs, and each chapter closes with a 'spot guide', outlining the key points to remember from that chapter.

Distance and open learning courses tend to attract more than their fair share of jargon. Even the descriptions of such courses can be confusing: distance and open learning, flexible learning, e-learning, remote study, all might refer to essentially the same type of course. However your course is described, you can be sure that this book will be relevant if you are studying in any way other than in a classroom with face-to-face contact with a lecturer. It will also be helpful if only part of your course involves open or distance learning. Traditional college and university courses can involve an element of distance and open learning, perhaps when you are asked to undertake a career research module, or if a major project is to receive little supervision beyond the material that has been placed on the internet to guide you. If you are undertaking a vocational course, you might find your time divided fairly evenly between face-to-face studying and distance and open learning. This can be disorientating, particularly if you had not anticipated this element in your learning structure, but this book will help.

As technology develops, so too does the exploitation of the potential of distance and open learning. Lecturers on traditional courses, where teaching and learning have customarily been based upon face-to-face situations, are increasingly being urged to use internet-based software to support their students in a wide variety of learning contexts, and this trend is set to continue. The danger for students perhaps lies in an overreliance on technology by course designers, who might assume that all students are happy with the prospect of an element of distance and open learning within a primarily contact-based course. The guidance offered here will help you to master this element of your course by showing you the study management techniques that you can employ in order to succeed.

The emphasis within this book is resolutely practical. When you are faced with a new situation, or begin to feel that you are losing control over your learning, four factors tend to make the problems worse and these are considered below.

You assume that you are alone

Of course, you cannot really be alone in the difficulty that you face: this book would not exist if no student ever encountered difficulties. However, working in relative isolation can lead to a creeping feeling that your problem is unique, or it is so minor that it is not worth bothering your tutors or mentors with it. This is not the case. Any problem that you face will not only be common to several other students on your course, it will always be valid enough for you to seek help. A minor problem can impede your progress in so many ways, having an impact on your work that is out of proportion to the size of the initial problem itself. By checking the troubleshooting guides and index of this book, you will see that your problem is not only recognised, it is also surmountable. Even if you need more individual help once you have followed the advice offered here, at the very least you will be able to ask for help with more confidence, knowing that you have worked some way towards a solution yourself.

You are concerned that you will get behind

One of the most intractable problems on a distance and open learning course is the fear that you are working at a slower rate than your fellow students. On many courses, this does not matter in the least: they are designed to allow you to work at your own pace and within your own time frame. However, even if you are simply working within your own parameters, determined to complete a particular module by Christmas, or hoping to tackle an assignment by the end of the week, coming across a problem that slows down your progress can do more than simply distort your timetable: it can leave you feeling that you will always be lagging behind on your course, however hard you try to catch up. Identifying your specific needs is paramount if you are to improve your learning and management techniques. This is not always easy once you feel that you are already behind. You might assume that you are not experienced enough, or skilled enough, to keep up with your course, but in reality the underlying problem is likely to be far more specific and relatively easy to overcome. Until you employ techniques to tackle reading lists, you might believe that you are just not reading fast enough to keep up. If you have not developed skills in researching on the internet, you might waste hours of your valuable time fruitlessly wading through material and then find that you are behind with your other study tasks. In both these cases the answer is simple enough: it is merely a case of putting into practice the simple management techniques that will allow you to work at your most effective when under pressure. As well as helping you to develop new skills, this book will also reveal your existing strengths, highlighting those areas in which you already have a substantial skills base. You will then find the guidance in Chapter 4 especially useful in helping you to achieve your study targets.

You are uncertain about the course advice being offered

However clear the guidance you are offered is intended to be, you can still feel unsure about what is being asked of you and the ways in which you are expected to face each new challenge. For example, you might be anxious about the level of support you will be offered as you approach your first assignment, or be uncertain about how essential a residential study workshop is to your particular needs. Perhaps you are unfamiliar with the terms being used to describe aspects of your course or the studying process, or you are beginning to feel that the course is not exactly matching up to your initial understanding of what you would be doing. Receiving more and more advice from the same source does not necessarily make things clearer, and you will have a natural reluctance to keep returning to your tutor with what you feel might be minor worries, particularly if your concerns are hard to pin down and difficult to put into words, and you have limited contact time with your tutor. Chapter 3 will be useful here, and the advice offered in Chapter 5 will support you as you work towards a clearer understanding of what is expected of you and a firmer grasp on your own studying techniques. In Chapter 6 you will find a guide to assessment within distance and open learning courses. Methods of assessment are not always made entirely clear to students on courses, and this chapter will help to reassure you as you prepare to focus on the essential tasks before you.

You begin to doubt your core skills

Distance and open learning, like any other sort of learning, is essentially about exploiting the talents and experience you already possess and challenging you to develop new skills and a wider understanding of your subject. This sounds fine in theory, but your existing skills base can be obscured by the new demands being placed upon you. You can become so concerned to prove yourself in this new learning situation that you simply forget that most of the tasks you are being asked to undertake are simply repackaged versions of challenges you have already faced at one time or another. Chapter 6 will be essential as you assess your present skills and plan, in a positive way, to move forward. One underlying problem can present itself in a variety of ways, and this can be disconcerting. On one module of your course, for example, you might feel unprepared for each assignment, find you cannot fully grasp the reading material you have been offered and then find you are late with an assignment. You will feel as if you are failing on all levels, lacking in the key skills you need to succeed in your course, yet the fundamental problem might be as simple as a change in your routine that has forced you to cram most of your studying into the weekends, rather than allowing you more time to reflect on what you have learnt and develop your ideas naturally. Chapter 8 will go some way towards helping you to identify problems such as these, which can be surprisingly difficult to spot without help, and will offer solutions that are both practical and manageable within your circumstances.

Despite these potential difficulties, this book is not designed simply to support you as you face a crisis. Although it will help you in identifying your problems and resolving them in the most practical, time (and labour) saving way, it will also encourage you to develop a more proactive approach to your learning situation. Producing a personalised timetable, for example, is one way of working through an existing timing crisis, but it is far better used as a tool to prevent the crisis in the first place. If you can develop the skill of reading productively, make relevant connections between diverse areas of study, and work in a positive way with your tutors, understanding that this is a two-way relationship in which you have a say, you will pre-empt problems before they can arise. This is perhaps the most valuable use you can make of this book: you can manage your course, remain in control and exploit each learning opportunity to the full; it simply takes strategic thinking and a positive, proactive approach to the challenges that lie ahead of you.

2 The Right Course for your Needs

Troubleshooting guide

Use this chapter for help if:

- you are choosing a distance and open learning course
- you want to take an overview of your course
- you want to assess whether your course is right for your circumstances
- you are beginning to think about learning strategies
- you are planning your finances
- you are studying as part of your continuing professional development
- you are wondering how to fit your studying into your domestic life
- you are working professionally whilst you study

You may already have chosen your distance and open learning course, but it is still a useful exercise to work through the factors involved in making such a decision. This will help you to analyse the strengths and weaknesses of your chosen course, and the impact that it might have upon your life; it will also prepare you for making choices between further courses in the future. Within this chapter several key issues will be explored: your financial commitment to a course, the ways in which your course can help you to further your career, the academic value of your course and the impact that it will have upon your domestic situation. Each of these factors will have a bearing, to a greater or lesser extent, upon your decision to commit to a particular course of study, but first it is helpful to define what is meant by distance and open learning.

Distance and open learning

The ways in which courses are labelled as either 'distance' or 'open' learning can be confusing, and frequently there is no difference between the two: the terms have become interchangeable in most learning situations. To add to this potential confusion, other terms have been coined in order to describe what are essentially distance and open learning courses: e-learning, flexible study, remote access courses, open-ended modular study. Again, these are essentially new labels for distance and open learning courses, and the fundamental elements of the study situation will remain the same, with only minor variations in the way in which some aspects of the courses are delivered or assessed. In addition to courses that are clearly based upon distance and open learning, some traditional courses incorporate elements of distance and open learning, sometimes in a rather haphazard way, with students being unclear as to which modules are to be taught in a traditional way and which will be reliant upon distance and open learning techniques.

In order to cut through the confusion, there are several basic features of distance and open learning worth bearing in mind, before we move on to considering how you might compare one course with another, or assess the relative strengths of your chosen course. In the most general terms, distance and open learning courses offer:

- *Distance rather than face-to-face learning situations:* this is, of course, the most obvious point of difference between a site-based course, with face-to-face lectures and tutorials, and a distance learning situation. The distinction is clear, but do not assume that all distance and open learning courses involve no more than a token face-to-face element. Some contact learning is built into many distance and open learning courses (such as study workshops or weekend schools) and you may well be able to develop your own contact time, arranging sessions with your tutor or supervisor or planning study workshops or discussion groups with fellow students.
- *Bulk delivery of materials*: although this is not always the case, there is a tendency within distance and open learning courses for students to receive the bulk of the learning material at the outset of a course. This is to some extent due to the technology used to deliver the course (a whole website might be accessible to each student at the outset) and sometimes it is due to the logistical demands of distance learning (it is far more efficient to send a complete course handbook and pack of study material to a student than send it out piecemeal as the course

progresses). Whereas undergraduates on campus might be offered only the reading list that relates to one term's work, and will sit in on lectures at a manageable pace, distance and open learners are more likely to be faced with a whole year's worth of material at once. This may seem like a minor point, but it is worth remembering as you begin your course: it can be extremely disconcerting to face so much material at once, and you will have to keep reminding yourself this is just another way to deliver the material you need, and you will have time to work through it at a reasonable pace.

- *A varying work pace*: this is a crucial difference between some distance and open learning courses and more traditional, contact-based courses. Whereas an on-campus course is usually planned on the basis that a group of students will all be studying at roughly the same pace, handing in assignments at the same time and attending group lectures and seminars, a distance and open learning course can be organised quite differently. If the course is entirely flexible, perhaps because it is based predominantly on learning via the internet, each student is in a position to complete each module at an individual pace, perhaps completing self-assessment exercises that can be monitored as the student moves on to the next module. Even with courses that are designed to include some face-to-face interaction, it is often possible to 'dip' in and out of modules, revisiting sections of study as necessary and only moving on when the student is ready for the next stage. One word of caution here: although it is possible for some distance and open learning courses to be truly flexible, never assume that your course will be organised in this way. You need to be sure about deadlines for the completion of assignments or assessments and any other time constraints that are built into your course.
- *The use of technology*: distance and open learning courses necessarily rely increasingly upon technology, in the form of online research databases, CD-ROM material, internet-based learning centres and email contact between tutors and students. Designers of contact-based courses are also aware of the benefits to be derived from technology as a teaching and learning tool, but within distance and open learning technology can be crucial. However, even the greatest technophobe need not be discouraged: all designers of distance and open learning courses that rely upon technology are acutely aware of the need to make their courses as accessible and user-friendly as possible. Even if this aspect of a course puts you off initially, it is worth overcoming your reluctance and exploring the options more fully: IT courses can be offered as an integral part of a course and IT support is often plentiful

and available throughout the duration of your course. The great benefit, from your point of view, is that your course and all its supporting material will be available online, as and when you need it, 24 hours a day.

- *The chance to use your experience*: it is a myth that most distance and open learning courses are vocational, but the format certainly lends itself to vocational training that can be incorporated into the professional life of a student. Continuing professional development (CPD) courses are available in abundance within the distance and open learning sector, and they often require you to use your own experience in order to support your learning development. It is self-evident that every student, at every level, will be asked to use their own experiences to some extent, regardless of the format of the course or the subject being studied. However, within a distance and open learning environment you are more likely to be asked to work on your own initiative to identify the relevant experience and skills that you bring to the course. This need not be a hurdle, it simply means that you will have to analyse your skills and experience as you progress (Chapter 6 will help with this) and develop techniques for employing these in the most effective way to support your learning.
- *The development of your learning strategies*: again, each student on any course has to develop learning strategies that will cope with each new situation, but within a distance and open learning course you will need to adapt your existing learning strategies to suit what may be an unfamiliar learning situation. If you have not studied for some time, this prospect might be quite daunting. The key to success is to remember that you already have embedded learning techniques (you just need to use this book to help you to identify them) and that these will not be wasted, rather, you will be working to adapt them to meet a new challenge. Instead of making use of regular contact time with tutors in order to assess the value of your strategies and compare them to those employed by your fellow students, you might need to analyse them and adapt them in relative isolation. However, you will find that self-assessment exercises on your course will help, as will study chat rooms on the internet, as well as working through the guidance offered within this book, particularly in Chapter 5 where your learning experience will be analysed and methods for improving your learning techniques will be suggested.

Naturally, anyone involved in the delivery of distance and open learning courses could add to this list of key features or refine them, but this will give you a broad understanding of how the term is generally understood and used within the confines of this book. For many people embarking on a distance and open learning course for the first time, the process can be daunting, and their confidence in what they are about to do can be undermined by some popular (and now rather old-fashioned) misconceptions about this type of course.

Having offered some criteria that define distance and open learning courses, it is therefore also worth pointing out what they are not:

- *Less academic*: distance and open learning courses are not an 'easy option', in that they are not necessarily any less highly academic than any other course. The debate about vocational and academic training and their relative merits will continue for some time, and you will naturally choose a course that suits your requirements, but you can feel confident that you are not enrolling on a course that is setting lower academic standards simply because it is a distance and open learning course. What *might* be easier about such a course is the way in which you are able to approach it. If you have been out of education for some time, a full-time, full contact academic course might be unattractive to you, not in terms of its content but in terms of the timing and delivery of the course. You may feel that you will be thrown into demanding academic situations that are too unfamiliar for you to be able to cope easily with them. A distance and open learning course might allow you more time to develop your academic skills; it is for this reason that many students have found such courses to be a useful way back into full-time or contact-based higher education.
- *Less rigorous*: this is certainly not true of distance and open learning courses. Indeed, they can be far more rigorous than more traditional courses, in that we all tend to be far more exacting of ourselves than others are in their judgements of us. Although you may have more time to develop your work on a distance and open learning course, the resulting work that you produce will be assessed as rigorously as any other comparable work produced by any other student. In addition, the ease with which some distance and open learning courses can be designed to allow for frequent self-assessment can lead to a far greater rigour within the course.
- *Less flexible*: although the flexibility of distance and open learning courses has already been stressed, and this is one of the most attractive features of such courses for many students, at the outset they can sometimes seem to be less flexible than contact-based courses. You might be faced with a course itinerary that seems less open than you had hoped, includes apparently rigid deadlines for each assignment and

seems to allow for little adaptation as your course progresses. This will not normally be an accurate reflection of your course as a whole. Course designers will attempt to impose some structure on the course outline and itinerary so that students can see the 'ideal' way of progressing through the course, but there will always be some flexibility built into the system. Similarly, students will be offered a standard route through the course, outlining the most complementary and popular module or block options, but this does not necessarily preclude the possibility of changing your module options as your course progresses. As with many aspects of your learning experience, you will need to move through the course with an open mind and ask about variations as your work develops, never assuming that what you have been given is the only way forward.

- *Less well supported*: in one obvious sense this is true. Students on a campus-based course will be surrounded on a daily basis with fellow students who will be supportive, answer queries and discuss the work being undertaken. If they have a problem they can drop in on a tutor for a chat and their departmental secretaries will be on hand to help them cope with many aspects of their courses. However, in reality the picture is often quite different. Universities and colleges have long vacations, during which students are often faced with placements or the writing-up of dissertations, and support during these times can be scant. Many undergraduates complain of a feeling of isolation, despite working on a busy campus. For the distance and open learner the support can be constructed in such a way as to provide regular and timely help. There will be a support structure set in place by the course provider; this might involve web-based chat rooms, message boards and real-time email support via the site. There may also be face-to-face sessions at regular intervals. In addition to this each student can expand and strengthen the support structure by forging study partnerships with other students, whether on a face-to-face or email basis, or form discussion groups, either on the internet or through regular, informal meetings of students. Chapter 5 offers further guidance on how your support structures might be put in place and maintained for the duration of your course.
- *Less recognised and valued as qualifications*: there is no reason why a distance and open learning course should provide you with a qualification any less well recognised than any other course, but you do have to be careful when choosing a course. There is such a proliferation of courses in some areas of study that it can be difficult to choose between competing courses. There are several clues that will help to guide you

through this potential minefield. Firstly, check the credentials of the course provider: is it a well-recognised institution? Then check how long the course has been running. You need not be put off a course simply because it is relatively new, but you will want to check the validity of one that has only recently been set up. Lastly, find out where this course can take you. Is it recognised by other institutions to whom you might apply for further courses in the future? Is it recognised by your professional body? Once you have worked through these questions, you will be in a good position to make a judgement about whether it is worth investing your time and money in the course.

- *Less pressurised*: sadly, this is not true, except in the sense that you might gain some flexibility over the timing of your study. As with a campus-based course, you will have deadlines to meet, assignments to prepare and assessments to master. Whether or not you find a distance and open learning course more pressurised than a more traditional course will depend largely upon the sort of student you are. Some students relish the chance to work within their own timetable, at a pace that suits them, and find that they are more productive when tackling courses of this sort. Others find the self-discipline required of them by a distance and open learning course almost impossible to master, and quickly become demoralised without the support of others around them who are also studying. Although you can never know for sure how you will react until you have studied on a distance and open learning course, there are questions which you can ask yourself that will give you some clues. Do you tend to work better alone rather than in company? Do you react well to deadlines, not letting them intimidate or fluster you? Are you naturally well organised, able to fit work tasks to the time available? Are you methodical in your approach to studying? Do you find communication easier by email than face to face? Do you have an overriding interest in your subject area that will sustain you throughout your course? If you answer 'yes' to these questions, you can be fairly sure that you will flourish on a distance and open learning course, but even if you answer 'no' to some, or are unsure of how you react to this type of challenge, there is no need to be put off. It will simply mean that the advice in this book, particularly in Chapters 4 and 5, will be of great value to you as you work towards becoming a successful distance and open learner.

When you are choosing a course, or evaluating the course on which you have already enrolled, it is a useful exercise to visualise key aspects of distance and open learning as they might relate to you. Every one of these

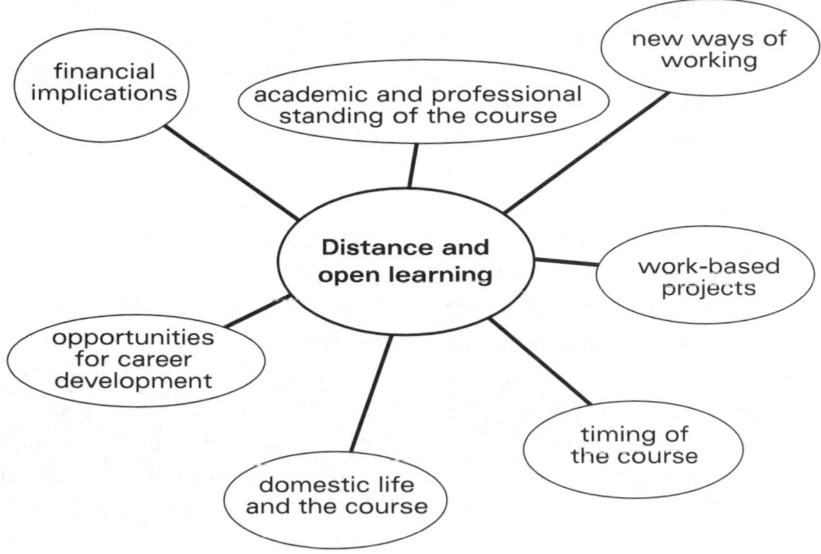

Figure 2.1 Key aspects of distance and open learning

elements will not be equally important to you, but each of them might have a bearing on your management of the course (Figure 2.1).

The financial implications of studying

There are three principal factors to take into consideration when considering finances and your course: how much will it cost directly? How much might you expect to pay in indirect costs? How much financial benefit might you derive from it in the future? These are fairly obvious considerations, but a surprising number of students fail to take account of them all, so it is worth exploring them here.

1. *How much will it cost directly?* You will be aware of the course fee, naturally, but in your planning try to take into account the best way to pay for the course. The fact that you can pay in instalments is not always made clear until the last moment, yet this could be the best way for you, spreading the cost just as you spread the learning. If your course is expensive, you might consider a career development loan, or a long-term loan spread over the duration of the course: find the cheapest

source of financing the course at the outset, to save you expensive credit bills in the future. If a course looks expensive at first, remember that campus-based courses at universities and colleges are subject to increasing tuition fees: this might make the distance and open learning option more attractive. Do not ignore the possibility of financial help in covering the costs of your course. You may apply for a course simply because it interests you, and so feel that nobody would be keen to support you financially, but it is a good idea to check whether the institution providing the course offers any financial support, either directly or in the form of inexpensive loans. Your employer too might be able to help. Even if a course is not directly relevant to your job, some employers take the view that any additional training is a good thing in their workforce, and set aside money to support their employees' courses. Your employer might be able to claim tax relief on this cost, which might make it a more attractive proposition. You might also be able to argue the case that, although your current course is not entirely relevant to your job, the courses that it could lead to in the future would be of benefit to the organisation. It may seem like a long shot, but it would be frustrating to find that you have missed the chance to receive financial help.

- *What might be the indirect costs?* Although you would expect this to be made clear to you at the outset, it is possible for course providers to overlook essential financial facts, so it is sensible to check out all possible extra costs. Are any residential sessions going to be held locally, or will you have to travel and pay for accommodation? Are you already accessing the internet in the cheapest possible way? If you will be asked to give presentations or demonstrations, will you have to bear the cost of materials? Will you be expected to attend conferences at your own expense? Is the book list you have been given exhaustive, or will you have to buy more books or journals as the course progresses? Perhaps most important of all, where will this course lead? It might not be too expensive in itself, but if it leads on naturally to another course that it will be necessary for you to take, how much will that cost? If it can be converted into a higher level qualification by the addition of, for example, a dissertation or more extended period of study, how much will this cost?
- *What future financial gain can you expect to make?* The answer to this might be 'none', if you are doing the course purely for your own satisfaction. However, if you are undertaking a course as part of your professional advancement, you need to be clear about the benefits and balance these against the costs. This is not necessarily a case of count-

ing the direct cost of the course, but more a question of any loss of earnings as a result of your course. You might assume that this will not happen, that your employer will allow you to take the occasional day off for studying or face-to-face sessions. However, if your course is prolonged, you might find yourself in the situation faced by many distance and open learners who use up their holiday for study time but then find that they desperately need a break and so have to take unpaid leave as well. It is worth bearing in mind whether this would be possible, and financially viable, for you. Exploring the professional benefits of your course will become important to you and so will be considered here in depth.

Career development through your course

Distance and open learning courses have moved a long way from their early stages, when they were divided between Open University courses, many of which were purely academic, and career development courses offered by professional bodies and academic institutions with an interest in a particular field of study. Now most universities and colleges have seen the advantages of distance and open learning courses, both in the revenue they can generate but also, as importantly, in the way in which such courses can broaden and enrich the student body of an institution. With such a range of courses on offer, it is essential, if you intend to use your course to further your career, that you make the best possible choice. There are several steps you can take to ensure you have all the information you need to make that choice:

- *The professional standing of the course*: this is often quite easy to ascertain. Check your professional journals and look not only at the adverts for courses, but also check articles that mention these courses or any editorial comment upon then. If the course is to be at postgraduate level, and is relevant to your first degree, go back to your undergraduate tutor or your university Careers Advisory Service and listen to what they have to say. Check the professional and academic accreditation of the course: as with first degrees, employers tend to ask about the body providing the course as much as the course content. If it is an NVQ course, there will be dedicated websites designed to help you to understand the nature of the course and the ways in which it might work within your career development.
- *Be aware of legislative changes*: if your course is leading you towards a

professionally recognised affiliation or qualification, it is worth checking whether any legislative changes in your area of work will make the course redundant or less valuable to you, particularly if it is a long-term course. In addition, it is a good idea to check with your professional body about any changes in entry or advancement requirements it intends to make in the near future.

- *Listen to personal recommendations*: although this is not an infallible way to choose a course, it is the only way to understand fully the inner workings of the course and the ways in which it is likely to impact upon your working life. You will not simply take such advice at face value without any further research, but you can be fairly sure that it is a worthwhile course if several of your colleagues are recommending it. It is surprising how often prospective distance and open learners fail to do this, hesitant, perhaps, about discussing a course until they are sure they can handle the workload, but it is the best way to get the inside information on a course and its value to you professionally.
- *Ask about the professional demands of the course*: course providers sometimes assume that these are obvious. If they are providing a course in advanced educational theory, for example, they might presume that only experienced teachers will apply, yet the course might be of interest to occasional trainers, or managers wanting to learn more about training and mentoring their staff. Do not be caught out by the small print: there may well be some leeway offered to students who do not fit the conventional mould, but you need to discuss this in detail before you commit to the course. If it involves any sort of fieldwork, you will have to make your circumstances clear to the course providers so that you can discuss how you are going to fulfil the requirements of the course.
- *Be sure about the studying requirements of the course*: one of the best ways to get to grips with the reality of the course (how much time you will have to devote to it, how much of your professional experience will be relevant, the chances of successfully completing it) is to do some research on the internet. Course sites often give pass rates and details of students who have taken the course in previous years as well as, in some cases, the professional standing of those students before and after the course. Beyond this, some course providers will allow you guest access to the whole course site for a limited time, and this will allow you to view the course materials in more detail and, more importantly, to eavesdrop on chat rooms or message boards for the site, so that you can see the course in action.
- *Discuss finances with your employer*: although you may not expect to

receive financial support from your employer, by discussing your plans you can ascertain how much flexibility you might be offered in terms of extra paid leave for studying, or financial support in the future if you intend to pursue further courses. Indirect costs, such as internet access, stationery and travel expenses, might be funded in part by your employer. Naturally it is useful to be clear at the outset about any long-term financial benefits you might derive from your course in terms of salary or promotion.

- *Use your tax advantages*: remember that, even if you are not self-employed, there may be tax advantages in taking a course, as it might be deemed to be a legitimate professional expense that can be offset against tax. If this is the case, you might also be able to offset the cost of interest on the loan you have taken out to pay for the course, so it is worthwhile making enquiries.
- *Consider potential changes in employer*: if you are relying upon sponsorship from your employer in any form, you must be clear about the practical implications of such a deal. Are you expected to pay back the money if you move to a rival organisation within a relatively short space of time? Will salary increases be deferred because of your sponsorship? It might be worthwhile turning down minor sponsorship (such as extra paid leave, or covering indirect costs) if this leaves you free to advance your career more rapidly.
- *Discover the reputation of the course provider*: again, professional journals will be of help here, as will discussions with your professional body. In the case of more traditional courses, students tend to be concerned with the overall reputation of a university or college, and this is still relevant to you, but for distance and open learning courses it is the reputation of the department providing the course with which you need be more concerned. Distance and open learning courses are often run entirely by one department, which views the course as a stand-alone entity. Course providers can be passionate in their support of the course they have designed, but their efforts are not always adequately reflected in the more general literature produced by the university or college. You will need to ask your colleagues specifically about the reputation of the department with which you will be dealing, and check its credentials for providing such a course. For example, does it run other courses within industry? Are the lecturers well known and respected in your professional field? Do the graduates tend to perform well professionally? Does the department carry out published and respected research? This might seem like a lot of research to carry out even before you start a course, but it will be worth it for the confidence

you can then feel in the qualification you will gain and the reputation of those who are providing it.

- *Exploit networking opportunities:* we all network professionally; it is an established part of professional life and sometimes we hardly notice we are doing it. However, it is not always easy to network via a distance and open learning course that does not necessarily offer obvious networking opportunities. Yet if you are going to the expense and effort of undertaking a course, it is reassuring to know that you will have some opportunities to meet others in your field, discuss your future career plans and build up a useful list of contacts to whom you can advertise your new status and qualification. It is not the task of the course providers to do this, nevertheless it is a good idea to check whether your course providers hold regular professional or academic conferences, whether they encourage their students to publish (and will support you as you prepare work for publication) and whether the course is supported by the most eminent figures in your field.

There are many factors that you will need to consider when you are choosing a course for professional reasons. Although the research will take some time, it will bring you the benefit of knowing that you are on the right course, for the right reasons, and you can expect to get the right result for your professional advancement. Time spent now will avoid the possibility of future disappointments, and once you have convinced yourself that your course will meet your professional needs, you can focus on the studying without any lingering doubts.

The academic value of your course

The academic value you place on a distance and open learning course is an individual judgement. If you are interested in the subject, feel that it is well taught and has broadened your understanding in an area, then you will be satisfied with the results. If you add to this the broader skills base that you might derive from the course, you will feel that it has a value beyond simply enhancing your mastery of a subject area. However, there might be other considerations to take into account when you are making your judgement and these are discussed below.

Academic judgements can be subjective

Just as you will make a judgement based upon your academic experience and interest, so too will others, and their judgement might be subjective and thus should be approached with caution. If you are seeking advice about a course, try to get several opinions from those whose judgement you value, and ask them about their overall view of distance and open learning courses, rather than just the one for which you are applying. If they take a negative view of the process as a whole, it is unlikely they will shrug off that prejudice in the case of your course. If their academic experience is limited, they may be unaware of the advances in distance and open learning courses in the last decade or so, both in terms of course delivery and the reputation and standing of such courses. You will not want to ignore the advice of your friends and colleagues, but the final decision must be based upon a consensus of the advice you have received and your own view of the course and its merits.

Your wider skills base

Although you will be undertaking a course because you have an interest in the subject, and perhaps hope that it will advance your career, when you are making a choice between several similar courses, it can help if you differentiate between them on the basis of the wider skills development they offer. These might include presentation skills, team working techniques, greater support with IT skills, more opportunity to express your ideas in writing or verbally, a more supportive structure for you to develop methodical working and research methods and time management techniques. It is only by researching the structure and delivery of courses in detail that you can discover which course offers you the best chance to develop in areas other than the purely academic.

Reputation of the course provider

As with professional development courses, you can usefully research the reputation of both the institution and the department which is providing the course. This is not to suggest that there is necessarily a divide between professional development and academic courses – inevitably there is a valuable overlap between the two – but you might be asking different questions of a department providing a principally academic course. These might include quizzing it about the professional destinations of its past graduates, the number of academic conferences it supports, the provision within its library and the range of academic staff on hand to support the course. If you look through the various university guides that are produced each year, you will be able to gauge the undergraduate entry requirements to your subject area, and although this is not an absolute guide, it will give you some indication of the standing of the department within the academic community.

The entry level of students

In addition to checking the entry requirements for undergraduate courses, it is wise to ask about the entry level standards of your fellow students on the distance and open learning course. You need not be put off if there is no formal entry requirement beyond the most basic of GCSE qualifications or an assessment of prior learning or experience. This may be your reason for applying, but knowing about entry requirements will give you some clue as to the academic level expected on the course.

Course content and materials

It is unsafe to choose a course based on nothing more than a glossy brochure or a website advertisment. Before you commit to a course, ask for an outline that shows as much detail of the content and delivery as possible, including methods of assessment, books and articles, the level of face-to-face contact and the means by which a course provider intends to support the course, such as internet interaction, direct contact with a tutor via email and any residential study sessions. If you are offered a reading list with only half a dozen books for a year's course, or only the briefest outline of how the course is to be supported as it progresses, you would be right to be wary.

Where the course might lead

Even if you do not, at this stage, intend to continue beyond the course for which you are currently applying, discovering where it might take you is a good indication of the academic standing of a course. This is especially important nowadays, when course titles can be confusing. A 'diploma' or 'postgraduate diploma' can mean different things to different institutions, and it would be a disaster to undertake a course that you thought would allow you to move on to further study within other institutions, only to find at its conclusion that it is not a nationally recognised and accredited qualification. An NVQ is a nationally recognised qualification, but it might not always lead on logically to the next qualification you have in mind. Do not allow the provider to be vague about this. Ask specifically about any more advanced course in which you are interested for the future, and ask for confirmation in writing that this course, if you complete it successfully, will grant you access to the more advanced course of your choice.

For most distance and open learners, the decision to undertake a course is based on an enduring interest in an area of study and a real enthusiasm to achieve a qualification that recognises their talents and experience. This in itself is enough, but if you work through the points outlined here and do your research thoroughly, you can avoid the risk of feeling let down at the conclusion of your course, or finding that the course you have chosen is either too advanced, or not challenging enough, for you.

Your domestic life

This is, for many students, the single most important consideration when committing to a distance and open learning course of study, perhaps the principal reason why they are considering a distance and open learning course rather than a full-time or campus-based one. These courses have developed over the years in part because they can be integrated into our busy lifestyles, both domestic and professional. However, the fact that a course is carried out at a distance does not mean that it will have only a minimal impact upon your domestic situation. You will work through the implications of your studying on the rest of your life as your course progresses, and the guidance offered in Chapters 3 and 7 will support you as you make decisions and plan your study schedules. However, this is an aspect of your studying that you need to take into account even before your course begins, and it is possible that you might have overlooked some of the features of your course that might adversely impinge upon your home and work life.

Residential schools

You are unlikely to overlook the fact that residential study sessions of one sort or another will form part of your course, but there are details that it is useful to know in advance. These might include the location of the sessions, whether they are day or weekend schools, and whether you will have any choice over which location you attend. To cover all eventualities, you will need to know whether they are a compulsory part of the course. If unexpected domestic disasters prevent you from attending, will this jeopardise your chances of success? Will you be able to attend an alternative session later in the course? How much do they cost, either in additional tuition fees or travel and accommodation expenses? Do not worry about asking questions such as these at the beginning of the course. It will be clear to the course providers that you are not being negative or unenthusiastic, you are simply a well-organised student who likes to plan ahead.

Forms of assessment

The forms of assessment are going to be crucial to your planning and may play a large role in your decision-making process. If, for example, you know that your lifestyle allows you to work intensively in short bursts, but that there will be times when you will have to get by on the minimum amount of work, a system of assessment that involves weekly tasks is soon going to cause you problems. Although flexible timing is likely to be one of the features of a distance and open learning course that appealed to you in the first place, you will have your own timetable (as outlined in Chapter 4) and certain elements of your course will tend naturally to fall at certain times of the year. You cannot plan for this with complete certainty, but if a course asks that you produce an extended piece of work (perhaps a dissertation or in-depth research project) and this task is likely to fall during your busiest time of the year, you might consider another course, or at the least have a discussion with your tutor to see if the course modules can be adapted in any way to suit your circumstances.

Assignments

Beyond your assessed work you will have regular assignments to complete, including perhaps self-assessment tests, essays and progress reports. These will form a natural and regular part of your study pattern and it will be relatively easy for you to plan for them, but you do need to ensure that they are firmly embedded within your personalised timetable, and that your family are aware of the fluctuating pressures being placed upon you. Your personalised timetable will most usefully become more than simply a guide as you study, it will also become a valuable tool in your family life. If you can share your planning with your family, and include in your study timetable any pressing family commitments, you will have taken a step towards ensuring that your family feel included in the process and will remain happy to support you.

Work-based projects

Work-based projects offer a similar challenge. No work colleague or employer is going to be delighted to find you embroiled in work-based study for your professional development course when they have pressing commercial demands that require your undivided attention. Again, this need not be a problem, but communication is key to achieving a smooth transition between work and study. It is unlikely that you will be met with enthusiasm if you spend time each day bemoaning how hard your study workload has become, but you need to strike a balance if you are to receive adequate support at work. Let everyone concerned know as soon as possible (weeks in advance if this is practicable) if you will be undertaking a work-based project. This includes the colleagues who might have to cover some of your work, your manager, whose support will be crucial, and any clients who might be affected. Allow this to become a dialogue: rather than imposing your timetable on them, discuss how it might be adapted to suit everyone's needs.

Support from your colleagues

Even if you are not involved in work-based projects, you will be relying upon the goodwill and support of your work colleagues. Those closest to you will know about the course and your study plans, and will support you in a variety of ways, as long as you can be clear about the type of support you need, from help with internet searches to being left alone some lunchtimes to get on with studying. On another level, it is worth considering making your activities known to your wider circle of colleagues. If yours is a professional development course that would be relevant to some of your colleagues, you might run lunchtime seminars each month to pass on what you have learnt. If you know that your course will be of interest to others in your organisation, you might write an article for the company newsletter. This may sound like yet more work, and you might hesitate to push yourself forward in this way, but you will be pleased with the support you can garner from colleagues once they begin to understand what it is you are trying to achieve.

Availability of support

Chapter 5 will explore the ways in which you can enhance and strengthen your study support structures, but you need to know at the outset whether the regular support offered by the course provider is available at a time that suits your domestic situation. If you intend to do most of your studying at weekends or during the evening, will there be online support available when you need it? If you know that your study time will have to be planned in bursts, can you be sure that the response time for queries is fast enough to be of use to you when you need it? Can you contact your tutors by telephone out of office hours? None of these factors need put you off a course, but it will require more careful planning on your part if the support offered does not fit perfectly into your work and study routine.

Changes to your routine

No plan can (or should) be so rigid that it cannot allow for any flexibility as unexpected demands on your time arise. However, we tend to plan according to life as we are living it in the present, rather than how it might be in the future. When you develop your personalised timetable, you will need to take into account those activities that you know will disrupt your study routine (business trips, family holidays and so on) but you also need to scrutinise the outline of the course. If your work is seasonal, you will find it difficult to keep up with your studying if your traditionally busy time at work clashes with the most pressurised time in your course. If you expect to be moving house in the next year, or changing your job, try to incorporate the possibility for change in your timetable, even if you are unsure of the exact dates involved. Allowing some slack time within your personalised timetable, which can be moved about as necessary, might save you an enormous amount of pressure later.

Finance

The financial implications of your course have already been mentioned, but it is worth pointing out here that your financial plans need to be shared with your family. Although you may think this is obvious, and naturally you will discuss the cost of the course, it is the underlying costs you need to point out. It may be clear to you that a presentation is going to be expensive, because you have to buy the materials and travel to the venue, but it might be far less obvious to those around you. If you expect to have to take unpaid leave for a week at some point during your course in order to complete a major assignment, this is better discussed at the outset rather than coming as a nasty surprise later. As with the timing of your study routine, these are preliminary matters that need not be a problem in themselves, but can cause huge problems if you fail to open up effective channels of communication before your course begins.

Access to technology

Access to technology is a minor irritation for many students that can become a major problem if it is left unchecked. Unless you have several computers at home, all with CD-ROM facilities and broadband internet access, and unlimited personal access to the internet and email at work, you may find yourself battling for time on the computer. One of the benefits of devising a personalised study timetable is that you can be clear about your need to access a computer and this will then become part of your normal domestic routine. Any parent with school age children will be aware of the level of screaming that can develop once the computer is taken over by coursework, so make sure that you have resolved this issue before you begin your course.

Somewhere to study

Students vary in the way in which they like to study. Some people find it almost impossible to work in silence, hate studying in a library for this reason, and would much prefer to work at the kitchen table with the family around them. For these students, the presence of their family or friends acts as an unacknowledged source of support. For others, peace and quiet is crucial to productive working. You must analyse your most effective ways of working and decide which type of student you are. If you need peace and quiet, you will need to arrange a time within your family routine when you can be left undisturbed. This does not generally cause problems unless your family are unaware of your timetable or you have children under the age of six! If you cannot easily find space at home to study, you might have to alter your study times or accept that on occasion you will have to travel to the local library to work, or stay later at work so that you can study without distractions.

Time to study

Although distance and open learners sometimes lament the lack of time to study, feeling that life is crowding in on them and making studying impossible, it is more usually the case that they have problems with time management rather than physically having too little time in which to learn. Again, including your family in the preparation of your personalised timetable will help, but you also need to differentiate between different types of study time. Chapter 4 will cover this in more detail, but you will have three types of study time: regular time, wish time and extra time. Within your routine you will have regular slots for study. These may alter week by week, but you will know, for example, that six hours each weekend and two, three-hour sessions during the week will be spent on regular tasks, such as producing essays and reports or working through course materials. In addition to this, you will have 'wish time', time that you hope to spend on extra tasks, such as catching up on reading or visiting the online course chat room. It will not be a disaster if you miss this one week, but you know that, if no crisis hits you, you can be sure of spending several hours of wish time working through these tasks each week. Your 'extra time' will only be used if you are getting behind with your timetable, or if a deadline is approaching and you fear that you cannot meet it. Your family will know that this will happen only occasionally, and will make allowances, leaving you to work until the panic is over.

Additional study opportunities

You do not have to differentiate rigorously between your home life, work life and study life. You might work best with a level of compartmentalisation, but distance and open learners can overlook the obvious when it comes to melding the different aspects of their lives together. If you have to attend a conference, your colleagues might like to join you (and your employer might pay your expenses) and in this way you can strengthen your support network. If you have to attend a residential study session, you do not have to assume that this always means leaving the family at home. Although the chance to include work colleagues and your family into your course might be limited, taking such chances when they are offered could enrich your overall experience.

Taking time out

It can appear to your family, particularly if this is your first distance and open learning course, that they are being presented with a set of demands and restrictions. You need time to study, the family budget is paying for the course, you might be unable to keep up with some of your traditional family commitments. They might see the benefit in the long term of supporting you now, but you can easily demonstrate the short-term benefits that the course could bring. Although your timetable is principally concerned with times when you have to study, it should also include times when you absolutely, without a doubt, take time off. The importance of this cannot be overstated. Undergraduates take long vacations without giving it a thought, full-time postgraduate courses are rarely as full time as they might appear, but distance and open learners tend to work far harder than other groups of students, cramming each spare minute with study tasks and never feeling that they are getting ahead. A distance and open learning course is, by its very nature, infinitely expandable. You could spend hours each week on one piece of research and still be aware of the gaps in your knowledge: this is the permanent condition of the academic. It is vital that you use your personalised timetable to show you when you have completed a reasonable amount of work on each task, and then to make you move on to the next task. In between those two processes, you *must* take time out to rest and reflect on what you have learnt. This will make you a far less stressed member of your family and will actually help you to be a more productive, thoughtful and creative student.

Keeping everyone up to date

Your life can become so busy once you embark upon a distance and open learning course that it is easy to forget to keep your colleagues and, more particularly, your family up to date with what is happening. You will periodically be reviewing and adapting your timetable, and it is important to share these changes with everyone concerned, so that nobody is faced with an unexpected absence as you work through a timing crisis that they had not foreseen. The habit of discussing your progress and your plans becomes especially important as your course draws to a close. The support that you are being offered by your family might be dependent upon their belief that this is to be a short-lived interruption in the family routine, and can evaporate if you then announce that you intend to enrol on a further course without having mentioned this possibility to them. Although communication within your family will be natural to you, a distance and open learning course can disrupt normality, as you become more involved in studying and the demands of your course, and this can be divisive unless you make a conscious effort to talk through your routine and your plans as they develop and adapt.

In many forms of adult education a family life can be restrictive: it might have prevented you from attending a full-time course, or made on-campus courses prohibitively expensive. Once you embark on a distance and open learning course, you will see how positive it can be to have your family's support as you work through your course. The archetypal view of the distance and open learner, sitting up all night at the computer after a long day's work, frantically typing with one hand whilst eating with the other, is no longer relevant. We are all adept at multitasking, courses are now designed to take almost every eventuality into account, and your family and work colleagues will become the mainstay in your support system throughout your course. What is required of you is simply that you explain your needs to those around you, discuss how best to plan each stage of the course and keep open the lines of communication.

Spot guide

The key points to remember from this chapter:

- make an assessment of how well your distance and open learning course suits your needs and fits into your long-term plans
- take an overview of the advantages and challenges of your course
- identify the learning outcomes you intend to achieve
- analyse both the direct and indirect costs of your course in your financial planning
- consider every possible source of financial support
- include professional advancement in your course strategy
- planning and communication are going to be vital as you fit your studying into your professional and domestic life
- plan your study time and space at the outset of your course

3 Elements in Distance and Open Learning

Troubleshooting guide

Use this chapter for help if:

- you are unfamiliar with the teaching components of your course
- you are finding your initial workload daunting
- you are not sure how you work best
- you are unfamiliar with e-learning
- you are facing a one-to-one tutorial
- you are preparing to attend a day school or residential study school
- you want to make the most of your workshop and discussion groups
- you want to maximise every learning opportunity

▶ Course components

Distance and open learning courses will differ in the ways in which the learning process takes place. They range from almost entirely web-based learning, with only occasional one-to-one tutoring, to hard copy learning where student packs are sent by post and backed up by regular tutorials. Even within these variables, no two courses will be identical in their delivery, even if they are both using essentially the same course components. No one method is better than any other, although some subjects lend themselves naturally to the use of one type of course delivery rather than another. What is important is that you feel confidence in the course components you are making use of, they suit your learning style and are appropriate for the training being delivered. Most courses will combine several of the course components discussed here in order to maximise the potential of each. You may not be sure which learning style suits you best, but by working through the options as they are described below you will be able to gain a good idea of how you might be working within each component, always remembering that we can adapt our natural learning styles to suit new demands placed upon us.

Hard copy packs

What is involved

Information is sent to you in study packs, sometimes covering several modules of a course in one pack. The notes you are sent might include tutor instructions, sample assignments, course handbooks, copies of journal articles, reading lists and tutorial material. This can seem strange, as you will be reading material that would more usually be delivered within a lecture or seminar situation, but you will soon get used to this style of learning. Tutorial material is the basic learning block within this type of component, but this is likely to be backed up intermittently with references to videos that you should watch, or books and articles you need to study in order to support what is being taught.

The advantages

Because you are receiving so much material at once, it is easy to gain an overview of the way in which the course will unfold. It also allows you to check backwards and forwards in order to remind yourself of what you have already covered, or see how your current learning will fit into your future work. It can be reassuring to work with hard copy material: it can make the learning process seem more solid, somehow, because you have a work pack in front of you. It also allows you to work away from the computer or television, which can be useful if you intend to study away from home at times.

The potential disadvantages

Suddenly the course seems like an awful lot of hard work! What looked relatively straightforward in the course brochure or itinerary has suddenly become reality in the form of a huge study pack and you can feel rather isolated in these early days, wondering how you will cope with working through all the material.

Managing the learning process

Immediate organisation is essential with this learning component. In your initial rush of enthusiasm, there is the danger that you will open the study pack, look through it all, and then allow it to lurk, untouched, for a week or so as you summon up the energy to tackle it. You then run the risk of beginning to feel as if it is just too much material to cope with, and that you are beaten by the course before you have even begun. What you are being offered is the course in one package. Even if other course components are also being used, the study pack will form the basis of the learning and so may span the whole course, but it is not being sent to you in the order in which you will be required to use it. Splitting it up and organising it now will ensure that you are in control. Keeping separate files for reading lists, tutorial material, commentaries on videos and television broadcasts and notes on books and so on is fundamental and easily done.

As each type of material is filed away, you will have a clearer idea how you might begin to use the material, but it is also a good idea to work through it all briefly at this stage. Make a note of the books you are asked to read. If they are referred to frequently you might consider buying some of those listed on your reading lists. You can also begin to organise your first trip to the library: you will be able to use your local university library, even if you are not registered on a course with them, but this should be arranged now, rather than leaving it until you need access to a book in a hurry. Schedules of television programmes to watch can be written in your diary now, rather than having to keep checking back to the course pack, as can the dates of residential schools. This hard copy pack of materials will form the basis for your personalised study timetable, which will be discussed in more detail in Chapter 4. There is plenty to do even before you start to work through the material in a more concentrated learning mode. If you work on your personalised study timetable now, importing all the information you have been given in the pack, you will be clearer about the tasks ahead of you and less likely to feel overwhelmed.

Once you have worked through the material in this practical way, extracting what you need in order to plan your reading and your study timetable, it is a good idea just to browse through the tutorial sections of the pack. This should not be a detailed read through of all that it has to offer: this would take too long and could be distracting. It is more a case of dipping into sections throughout the pack, familiarising yourself with the style of writing (remembering that it might have been written by several tutors) and beginning to get an idea of the depth and breadth of the study areas. This will not take long, just an hour or two will be sufficient, but once you have browsed through it you will feel more confident about the learning you are about to undertake. From now on, you will probably be working through it in detail in a methodical way; you might never again dip into it like this, but you will remember the overall pattern of the course from this initial reading, which will help you to gauge your progress as your learning skills and knowledge develop.

Videos and audio cassette tapes

What is involved

This is obvious, but it is worth noting that video and audio cassette studying comes in various guises. You might simply be asked to watch a video of a play, film, documentary or scientific procedure. You might also be offered lectures on video or audio cassette. Each of these triggers a different type of learning experience, so you need to be prepared to vary your approach accordingly.

The advantages

Videos and audio cassettes offer a break from the more usual reading-based learning experience, and for this reason alone they can boost your recall and understanding. They also give you the opportunity to study in relaxed surroundings, which could be a problem if you are likely to fall asleep after a long day's work, but you can vary your study schedule so that the video or audio cassette forms a more relaxed, yet no less informative session to break up your other tasks. As with books and tutor packs, you can rewind at any point to review what you have just seen or heard.

The potential disadvantages

It can be difficult to persuade your family and friends that this really is studying, but you do need an uninterrupted time to view each video or listen to each audio cassette in its entirety so that you can grasp the overall picture of what you are being offered. Too many interruptions will break your concentration, so be clear about needing some space and time to work. There is also a temptation to see this as a 'soft option' in your study timetable, and it is in some ways, but beware of the danger of switching off because you have scheduled your viewing or listening for a time when you are too tired to take in the information.

Managing the learning process

Plan to view each video or listen to each audio cassette at least twice. We miss a surprising amount of information on a first viewing or listening: this is particularly true of videos that are principally designed to entertain, such as filmed plays or entertainment films. Making notes as you view or listen is going to be essential, but you might like to leave this until a second session, first getting your bearings and simply watching the whole video or listening to the audio cassette through once. Before you begin, make sure that you are absolutely clear about why you are watching or listening. Does this back up the tutor notes that you have been studying, in the form of a demonstration or experiment? Is it a taped lecture? Is it a documentary, perhaps as background material of a more general nature? If you are watching a play or film, are you approaching it from the most relevant critical angle? There is an enormous amount of material encapsulated in just a few minutes of video or audio cassette, and you could lose much of the value of this material if you are not fully prepared for the task ahead of you.

You have to decide whether you are expected to watch the video or listen to the audio cassette unaided, that is, relying solely on the knowledge you have already acquired, or whether they are to be used in conjunction with notes you are expected to read through as you watch or listen. In either case you will want to have the remote control handy to pause the video or audio cassette as you make notes, but it is worth practising with different techniques. Some students find it easy to read through the notes and supporting material and then watch the video or listen to the audio cassette without any further reference to this material whilst they make their own notes. Most find it easier to view or listen to a section (our usual concentration span for this is about ten minutes) and then pause whilst they refer back to any supporting material and then make their own notes on the section, sometimes having rewound the tape to study the section again. You will not know which method suits you best until you have tried several, but once you have discovered the best method for you, it will work for most of the video or audio cassette material that you are given.

Television and radio broadcasts

What is involved

As with video, the answer to this seems obvious, but you will have to bear in mind the nature of the broadcast. A video might be designed especially for your course, whereas a broadcast might be far more general in nature, designed to be used on several courses, or for general broadcast. The timing of the broadcast will give you a clue: a radio or television programme at two o'clock in the morning will be aimed at a specific audience, and this is often a studying audience.

The advantages

Broadcasts offer you a change in your studying pattern, a chance to take in information in a different way. Unlike videos, broadcasts might be part of a series of programmes, some of which are only indirectly related to your needs. If you enjoy one style of delivery, and find the programme really interesting, you will be able to check whether there are other programmes in the same series that you could watch just to get some more background material for your course.

The potential disadvantages

You may not know yet whether you learn well by either looking at the television or listening to the radio. Some students find visual learning easy, some find listening far more effective. Although this will not put you off this course component, it is most effective if you can discover which sort of learner you are. If you find it difficult to take in what is being said on the radio, you might consider the possibility of taking detailed notes (some students even take down a transcript of the entire broadcast on a laptop or download it from the radio internet site before working through it to make more concise notes) before you try to process the information. If you find the television distracting, and tend to look at the images at the expense of what is being said, detailed notes that can be condensed during a second viewing might help. As with video, you will not know how you learn best until you try, but as long as you remain aware of this as a potential problem, you will be able to overcome it. Whatever the case for you, it is never a good idea to test this out when you are tired. We have all been in danger of falling asleep during lectures, and listening to the radio or watching the television, sitting on your sofa, just increases this risk, so test your natural abilities only when you are fully alert and ready to learn. Timing can be a practical problem, in that programmes might not be broadcast at a time that suits you. Although videoing or taping (with a timer switch if necessary) is the easy answer, find out if your course provider has a lending library of videos or audio cassettes available, just in case you forget to record a programme or lose the tape or video.

Managing the learning process

As with videos, you will soon discover whether you are a visual learner and you will weigh the importance of broadcasts accordingly, using the methods suggested above to help you to retain as much information as possible. It is surprising how many programmes of a more general nature will be valuable as your course progresses, so make sure that family and friends are alerted to this possibility so they can tape programmes they think might be of interest to you. You will build up a library of videos, with the counter mark for each programme on the tape included on the label, but you will be working from your notes on these programmes as you work on assignments, rather than referring back to the programmes themselves too often. They are just the starting point in a learning process that you need to make your own.

CD-ROMs

What is involved

CD-ROMs are, at their most basic, little more than enormous books captured on CD. So, for example, you can find an entire 12-volume dictionary on CD-ROM, or the transcript of several years' worth of newspaper articles. What CD-ROM allows you to do with ease is to search for information in a way that is impossible with many book indexes. If, for example, you are looking at a bibliographical catalogue, covering books and journals written over a 20-year period in a particular subject, you would be able to search by author name, subject, language, date of publication and so on, and this is a fantastic way of finding obscure articles written by authors of whom you have vaguely heard, without being clear as to what they have actually written. More complex CD-ROM and DVD technology will allow you to interact via your computer or the television with the data in order to test your knowledge, develop your skills and work through technical processes.

The advantages

Again, this form of technology will vary your learning experience, allowing you to access data easily and assess your progress. The sheer volume of information that can be held on a CD-ROM or DVD is reassuring in itself; you will feel that you have a whole host of resources at your fingertips.

The potential disadvantages

This technology tends to be expensive (sometimes prohibitively expensive for students) and so access might be limited; you may need to use some CD-ROM material in the library rather than at home. It can also be maddeningly slow. Interactive DVD and CD-ROM technology is necessarily designed to lead you through a process step by step, so getting to the point that you are interested in can be a tedious task, particular with self-assessment, where it may be difficult to skip through the sections with which you are familiar to the point where you would like your self-assessment to begin. A more insidious problem can occur with CD-ROM technology: the whole process can become so fascinating that you can spend hours chasing up obscure leads, thoroughly enjoying yourself but actually producing very little information that you need to act upon. This may not be a problem: a little browsing is fun, and serendipity in finding articles and books is a good thing, but you need to discipline your searching so you do not devote too much fruitless effort to it.

Managing the learning process

You can ensure success with this course component by being crystal clear about what you want to get out of it *before* you begin. Know exactly which author you are searching for, or precisely the subject area that you need to cover, and give yourself a time limit on the CD-ROM. If you are working with interactive technology, do not allow yourself to become sidetracked by what it has to offer beyond what you intend to do in each session. As soon as you begin to feel uncomfortable, perhaps feeling that the self-assessment is beyond you at this stage, turn off your computer or television and seek help. It may be that you are accessing a higher level of self-test that is expected of you, or that you are working out technical processes that have not yet been covered on the course: this can happen more easily than you might expect and it can dent your confidence.

All this technology is designed to be as user-friendly as possible, but if you have not had a great deal of experience using CD-ROM and DVD technology, ask about training before you go too far. This will be available, either in face-to-face sessions or via self-learning software. Once you begin, try not to let yourself become so dazzled by the technology that you forget that, however impressive the software, it is never going to be any more than a tool within your learning process. It is there to be used as an integral part of that process, rather than leading you away from your main purpose of working your way through the course.

▶ E-learning

However useful you find CD-ROM and DVD technology, it is always limited by the amount of information that is stored and the ways in which the software is designed to allow you to access it, but it can be deceptive. It is common to forget that you are working through a finite amount of information, packaged in a certain way. It feels so similar to working online that you begin to assume that you can get everything you want from the technology, and then feel frustrated when you realise that it will not offer you exactly the data you had hoped for, in the format you need. This is one reason why online learning is becoming so popular. Whilst the general (and rather clumsy) term 'e-learning' can refer to a variety of learning tools, from CD-ROMs to DVDs to computer tutorials and self-assessment computerised modules, the focus in the following section is on online learning, that is, learning via the internet.

This type of learning experience can be broadly divided into two categories: independent and guided e-learning. Independent e-learning will largely involve your own work on the internet, looking up references, using search engines and accessing conferences and journals online. Guided e-learning involves using the website set up by your course provider to help their distance and open learning students to access information, receive feedback and interact with each other and the tutors.

Independent e-learning

The rise of the internet has transformed our learning methods, and in general it is a valuable tool for a distance and open learning student, but it can have drawbacks. Before you incorporate the internet into your studying scheme it is worth considering the following points.

Know what you want

Going onto the internet with only a vague idea of what you are looking for will inevitably lead to wasted time and a reduced return on your efforts, but this is not always immediately obvious. Spending a fascinating hour or so looking through a dozen of the million or so sites you are offered in a subject area can be pleasurable, but you must ask yourself whether it is really profitable. Instead of wandering aimlessly, make yourself a 'shopping list' of data you need *before* you go online. You might, for example, want to look up specific conferences or find out about journals that are available online. As these can work on a subscription basis, you will need to check with your tutor or fellow students whether a journal or conference site is worth paying for, or perhaps whether your course provider is already paying for it. It might be easier, and cheaper, to use the site to look up a table of contents for a journal for free, and then to access it on hard copy via your library. If you want to review the current position on your subject area, you might usefully look through the sites that purport to relate to it, but stick to reviewing sites rather than their detailed contents. If you access each site you will waste time working through lots of extraneous material. Take the time to check the titles and brief details of the first 30 or so sites that the search engine is offering you before you commit to dipping into any of them. The message boards on many sites are tempting, and can give you a good idea of how general discussion of your area is progressing, but being lured into contributing yourself might be counterproductive in terms of your time and effort.

Know how to get it

It all seems so simple at the outset. You want to look up the work of a particular expert in your field. You have her or his name, and a rough idea of what she or he has written on the subject, so you just type in the name as a search term, only to find that she or he has written a dozen or so books and contributed to many more, as well as speaking at conferences and writing journal articles. If this person is the clear leader in your rather obscure field and is therefore the best authority on everything you are doing, this need not be a hurdle to your progress. However, it would be unusual for this to be the case: it would be a better use of your time to find out in advance the exact website address of the particular article that would be most useful to you so you can access the information you really need as quickly as possible.

Remember that sites can change

We know that sites can change, but there seems to be a law of technology which dictates that the very site you last looked out, which you now realise will be vital to your assignment, has gone missing just at the moment when you need it most. Sites posted for just one purpose (conference proceedings, for example) are unlikely to change, although they may disappear in time (just at the wrong time) but established sites run by large organisations may change on a weekly or even a daily basis. Make sure that you can get back to a site easily (remember that you can add an interesting site to your favourite site list temporarily) and download or print off material you think will be vital.

Never assume that you are being told the truth

This is perhaps the most intractable problem when working with the internet. It is difficult to keep in mind that just because information is published on the internet, it is not necessarily accurate. Even if the facts are true, you cannot always judge what it is that you are not being told: the bias of any article will not always be clear to you. In addition, articles on the internet will not normally have undergone 'peer review', the system by which articles are scrutinised by academics before publication. This is not to suggest that you should discard the internet as being unreliable, but it makes sense to take the information and opinions being offered to you with a degree of caution. If it is important to your study, you can use the internet as a guide to an area of publication and then check hard copy journals or books in order to develop your knowledge.

Manage your time and resources
Although by now you will be aware of the dangers of wasting time browsing on the internet, you will also need to consider your other resources, such as the cost of connection and paper. The paperless world of study is not yet with us, and it is difficult to resist the temptation to print off reams of internet pages in the hope that some of the information will be useful to you in the future. You have to strike a balance here. There is an understandable urge to print off everything you can, but there is an equally understandable reluctance then to work through it on hard copy because there is so much of it. On the other hand, most of us are not very effective at working through text on the screen and making notes, so you will have to download some pages. The easiest way to cope with this is to devise a study system whereby you always print off pages and work through them in the same session. That way you will limit the amount you print and you will make it useful to you by sitting down and highlighting as you go. Hundreds of unmarked sheets will be relatively useless to you, whereas 12 marked-up sheets, perhaps attached to your own notes, will be of lasting benefit.

Information goes out of date
It will become second nature to you to check the date of any book or article and make judgements about its relevance and validity based, in part, upon this information. This is less easy with internet sites, where it may not be clear when the site was originally published or last updated. As with the veracity of the information or the bias of a site, this factor will not automatically put you off using a site, but you might not choose to rely upon it if you cannot be sure how up to date it is. Some sites you will get to know very well, and you might then feel confident about how often, and how reliably, they are updated. With others, you will adopt a more cautious attitude. When referring to websites within assignments, you need to make clear the full website address, the location of the page to which you are referring and, if possible, the date the site was published or updated. If you are only referring to a few sites in an assignment, it is a good idea to print off the relevant pages and include them as appendices. This will save your marker the trouble of trying to read your assignment alongside the internet, and it will overcome the problem of sites disappearing or being altered after you have written your assignment. If you are making frequent references to lengthy sections of many websites, so that your essay is more of a commentary on those websites than anything else, you need first to check whether this is acceptable. Given that assignments which simply refer the reader to a series of book chapters would not usually be accept-

able, it seems probable that your work might have to be restructured. If it is accepted in this format, the marker will have to be checking websites whilst reading your assignment and you need to confirm that your marker has the equipment available to do this: you may need to make special arrangements over the deadline for the assignment.

Guided e-learning

Most distance and open learning courses depend, to a greater or lesser extent, on some element of internet interaction. This is most usually facilitated by course providers utilising software specifically designed to create websites and interactive learning centres which can be produced easily and updated quickly. The advantages of this approach to e-learning are clear: even lecturers and tutors with little internet experience can create and maintain these websites, and distance and open learning students can access them in their own time and get a level of support, from tutors and fellow students, that was impossible before the advent of the internet.

The disadvantages of this type of e-learning are relatively few, but they can have a considerable negative effect on the management of your course. The first of these is not actually your problem at all, strictly speaking. These software systems can generate such a high level of enthusiasm amongst tutors that they deposit the information from every scrap of paper relating to their courses on the course website. I recently came across a course which, when downloaded and printed off, devoted over 500 pages to course instructions, reasons for the existence of the course, aims and objectives of the course and instructions as to how the course itinerary would work. Not a single one of the pages actually taught anybody anything; it merely told them about the sort of things they might learn and how they might be expected to learn them. The student who came to me having tried to use the site was having serious doubts about whether he should begin the course, even though he was clearly able to succeed. The problem was twofold: he had not yet developed the art of picking his way though such a site and only printing off vital pages, and the course providers had apparently forgotten that much of the information they were giving to students on these pages could have been given to them during the two-day introductory residential session they held, presumably for those students who had not let the website put them off the course. The point of this example is that both course providers and students need to remain aware that e-learning is simply a tool, and its effectiveness rests with the management abilities of both tutors and students.

The second potential disadvantage is the problem of misunderstanding what is on offer. A study chat room is sometimes the first place that distance and open learning students go when they have a problem, but unless it is run by a tutor on the course, who is on hand to reply to students' queries, you can waste time talking around a problem with your fellow students rather than going directly to a tutor and asking your question. This leads onto the next problem: that of spending too much time within the e-learning environment to the detriment of your other study tasks. The e-learning system is there to support your work, but it is not designed to replace the other tools of your course: the face-to-face learning, the books and journals you are using and the other forms of media available to you. You will need to assess each month, with the help of your personalised timetable, whether you are making the most productive use of the time you spend within the e-learning environment.

The last potential problem with e-learning is that you might be tempted to stray beyond the confines of your current study task, working through self-assessment tests for which you are not yet ready, or spending hours checking out links to other sites beyond your current needs. You have a limited amount of time to study, and learning to be an effective e-learner is going to be crucial to your success in managing your course. This will be easier if you remember these points:

- Never assume that what you see on the internet (even on your course site) is 100% accurate. If you have any doubts, check the facts with your tutor or in a hard copy book or journal.
- Ration your time on the internet to make it a separate and manageable learning block of time, just one tool in your learning tasks.
- When searching, always have a shopping list of information you need, rather than browsing in a disorganised way.
- Be firm about not straying beyond your current needs and understanding.
- Always print out the pages you really need, but beware of printing out too much. Remember that a site might change, or even disappear, overnight.
- The pages you print out are just the start of the learning process. Use them as you would a photocopied section of a book or article and make your own notes on them or highlight the sections to which you will need to refer in an assignment.
- Make a note of the complete reference to sites you might need to revisit later or intend to include in an assignment.
- See study chat rooms as a useful, but not infallible, guide to your course and the tasks you are being asked to perform.
- If you work well with a few other students on your course, consider

developing your own chat room so you can continue to support each other more easily throughout the course.

▶ Face-to-face learning

Students enrolling on a distance and open learning course often expect there to be no face-to-face learning at all, but this is not often the case. Your course might well offer face-to-face learning opportunities in a number of formats: one-to-one tutorials, day schools, residential study weekends, workshops and additional support sessions. If you are undertaking an NVQ course, the face-to-face interaction might be a key element of the course and so might be greater than you expect. Each of the teaching and learning situations you might encounter during your course is evaluated here and practical solutions are offered to potential problems.

One-to-one tutorials

The frequency and format of one-to-one tutorials will vary depending on your course, but you might have the opportunity once or twice a term to meet with your designated tutor (or a tutor who has marked an assignment) in order to discuss your progress, the route you might take next with your assignments and the resources you can exploit. For any student working on a campus this is an everyday part of their course, one that causes them no great concern. For distance and open learners it can be far more problematic. If you have been out of formal education for a time, the prospect of spending an hour or so with a tutor working through your assignment or discussing your progress on the course can be intimidating. It is going to be far worse in prospect that it is in reality, but working to the following guidelines will help.

Understand what is on offer

Why are you being given this opportunity? Is it a general session, or are you meeting a tutor specifically to discuss a mark you received or an assignment you are tackling? How long is the session, and can you alter the timing to suit your other commitments? Are you being asked to do any prepatory work before you meet?

Know what is expected of you

Although you will take with you the obvious things, such as a copy of your assignment if that is what is being discussed, you will also want to confirm what is expected of you in the session. Will you be asked in detail about progress on your other assignments? Will you be expected to discuss your plans for the rest of the course, or beyond it? How long is the session? Will you be asked to read your assignment aloud, or simply discuss the marker's comments?

Be proactive in your approach

Once you have the information to hand about how the session will be run, you can take some control of the process. Make a list of questions to ask, and never be embarrassed about asking the tutor to slow down whilst you make notes. Take your personalised timetable, so you can show how organised you are and discuss whether your targets are realistic. Rather than bringing up vague queries and concerns you have, take the time in advance of the meeting to analyse what, if anything, is worrying you about your course and write down your points for discussion. Find out if other students on the course are also meeting the tutor on the same day and arrange to meet them if you would find this useful.

Feedback your experience to the tutor

One-to-one sessions work best if they are viewed as just the first stage in a continuing dialogue between tutor and student. These sessions can be incredibly pressurised: even if you are given a whole morning with your tutor, there will not be enough time to cover everything. You can reduce this pressure to some extent by being organised in advance, but still you are both working through ideas and problems, both thinking on your feet and trying to cover every issue as quickly and effectively as possible, and there is a high chance that something will be forgotten, or only covered in part, however well prepared you both are. Once the session is over, you can feel rather lost, having been offered a vast amount of information in a short time, and knowing that you might not see the tutor again for several weeks. This problem is easily solved. After the session, spend some time writing out what you have discussed, noting the full details of the books that have been recommended or the ideas you discussed for your next assignment. Once you have written everything down, email your tutor to confirm the details. This need not be too formal, just an email to thank your tutor for the time you spent together, and confirming the details of what was discussed. There are several advantages of this approach. Firstly, your tutor is reminded that you are committed, organised and proactive in your approach. Secondly, it gives your tutor the chance to correct any mistakes in the feedback, such as dates of residential schools or the names of book titles and authors. Thirdly, and most importantly, it gives your tutor the chance to rethink what was said in a less pressurised situation, to work through the ideas and email back to you some additional thoughts and suggestions. This is a bonus and makes the whole experience infinitely more valuable from your point of view.

You may have one-to-one sessions with several different tutors during your course, and each session will vary in both the expectations placed upon you and your requirements of the tutor. Remember throughout these sessions that you can maximise their use to you by following these guidelines, and that any one of these tutors might become your supervisor for a more extended piece of research, if that forms part of your course. If you make the most of one-to-one sessions, you will be in a stronger position to choose a supervisor with whom you work well when you face this decision.

Day schools

Day schools can be every tutor's (and distance and open learning student's) nightmare. A day crammed with teaching sessions, a desperate struggle to fit in each session and the constant effort by tutors and students to make some individual contact with each other, to make the day as useful as possible. If your course offers day schools just once a term, or twice a year, the pressure is even greater. They are also, of course, your best chance to consolidate your learning and explore new avenues. There are ways in which you can maximise the benefits of these schools, but it takes advanced preparation and a high level of focused organisation on the day.

Get as much detail in advance as possible

If you know how many sessions will be running during the day, who is leading each session and what is likely to be involved, you will be in a much better position to take advantage of them. This seems obvious, but day schools are often run with little detail being offered to students in advance, which will hamper your ability to make the most of this opportunity.

Put failsafe practical arrangements in place

Again this might seem obvious, but you need to be sure about what will happen if things go wrong. Could your childcare be extended by a few hours if there is a social event at the end of the day school? If you are taken ill, could you book onto a similar day school in the future? If the school begins at nine o'clock, can they arrange accommodation for you the night before? How expensive will this be? Do you have a map of the campus on which the school is being held? Do you need to get there early so you can walk around and get your bearings? Will the university library be open, so you can look up some references in your lunch break? You will find your own questions, but make sure you have asked them in advance of the day, so you are free to focus on the task ahead of you once you arrive.

Plan your attendance at each session

A day school is as much about you proactively extracting and using valuable information as it is about the tutors and lecturers offering you information. If you sit passively through six or eight sessions, you will not only be exhausted, and potentially demotivated, you will also have a lot of work to do after the event, reordering your notes and trying to see how everything fits together. You can reduce this feeling to a minimum by preparing in advance. Consider each session, checking the details you have gained from the course provider or the website. How might each session fit into your current studying tasks? What questions might you ask in each session? If you are unfamiliar with some of the ground to be covered, is there reading (either in journals or on the course website) you could do to prepare? Do you need to change your schedule so you begin to prepare an assignment earlier than you had planned in order to get the most out of the day? Are any sessions optional? You will probably want to attend every session, but it is worth asking the question, particularly if you could use the time to meet one of the tutors face to face.

Decide how much individual contact you can expect to have

Having suggested that you might be able to meet with a tutor face to face on the day, you will probably find that this is not an occasion on which you will be offered much individual attention. You might look for gaps in the programme and contact a tutor in advance to ask if you might meet to discuss a specific issue over lunch, for example, but it is unlikely that this contact will be prolonged. However, you can impose your own structure on your 'free' time, with a list of tutors to whom you want to introduce yourself, a tour around the library, an informal meeting with your fellow students to set up a discussion group and so on. You will be able to achieve a lot in both the formal and the informal parts of the day, as long as you are organised and understand what you can reasonably expect to achieve.

Extend the experience beyond the day school

As with one-to-one sessions, there can be a feeling of anticlimax after a day school. You have worked incredibly hard for the day, enjoyed meeting fellow students and had some contact with your tutors, but then find yourself with a pile of notes that must be analysed and sorted, and half-made arrangements that must be confirmed. This will take some time, so make sure you include these tasks within your personalised timetable. You might also consider ways in which the benefits of the day school could be extended. Have you now got a contact list for students working on similar assignments? Did you spend the evening after the day school discussing your ideas with students who might form a study group? Do you need to follow up leads about conferences that a group of you might attend? If you work through some of these possibilities, you will have extended your experience in such a way that a day school is the start of your next learning experience, rather than being an isolated feature of your course.

Day schools are always hectic events, and they can be a bit bewildering until you get used to them. If you minimise confusion by planning ahead, you will find that they can form the cornerstone of your course. Any distance and open learning course can leave you feeling remote from the tutors and your fellow students; a day school will lend substance to your learning process by reminding you that this is a 'real' course, with other students like you and a structure that will support you as you progress. They may not always be a compulsory part of the course, but they will never be a waste of your time if you make the most of them.

Residential study weekends

In essence, the guidelines for day schools also apply to weekend study schools, but there are several other factors that might come into play.

Cost

You may have taken account of the cost of residential study in your course plans, but do not assume that the cost need be prohibitive. If you find it too expensive for your budget, talk to the course organisers, as there may be funds set aside to help with the costs for some students. In your planning, try to work out the costs in advance, not just for the school itself (this will usually be included in the overall course fee) and the accommodation, but the cost of books that might be on sale during the weekend and the cost of socialising. Some basic budgeting in advance will prevent any nasty surprises during the event.

Your family

The cost to you might go beyond the financial demands of the weekend. If you have a family you might be including the cost of childcare, but you also need to take into account the effect on your family of your absence. Even the most supportive members of the family might feel unexpectedly threatened by the event, and a few rushed and excited telephone calls from you during the weekend are unlikely to help. If you then return home with a list of backup tasks that eat into your family time, you will be exacerbating the situation further, quite unintentionally. Talking through the study school in outline with your family before the event is essential, and reworking your personalised study timetable to take account of any new demands resulting from the experience will ensure that all members of your family remain on your side. Similarly, make sure your work colleagues know that you absolutely will not be available during the school, but you will be happy to share your new knowledge with anyone who is interested, perhaps through a workshop session at work the following week.

Socialising

This is a tricky issue. On the one hand, you will want to meet your fellow distance and open learning students, on the other hand, you do not want to waste valuable study time, and you might feel intimidated at the thought of meeting so many new people in a short space of time. This problem might not be resolved by your first residential school, if different sets of students are mixed together at each school. There might be relatively restricted time available for socialising (evening sessions are often run to complement the daytime sessions) and you will want to make the most of this time. This can take some preparation, particularly if you feel anxious about socialising in this way. Residential schools often make this easier by running informal social gatherings around a theme, a bit like workshop sessions but with the emphasis on casual discussion and the sharing of ideas rather than more structured tasks. However, you will want to work to your own agenda as well. Keeping up your contacts as your course progresses will help you here: make contact with a few of your fellow students in advance so you have people to meet rather than wandering around alone. It can be useful to arrange your own disucsssion group on one of the evenings. If you are expected to socialise with the tutors, remember that they need some relaxing time too and might want to talk about something other than your course. This is not a test where you have to set out to impress at every moment, instead it is a chance for you to build relationships, and it can be a useful way of meeting tutors, any of whom might later become your supervisor for an extended piece of work.

Exhaustion

This feature of residential schools is often overlooked: they are tiring experiences, for tutors and students alike. For this reason, it is not always a good idea to save your most important query for a tutor until the last night, when everyone is tired. It is also worth considering whether you can take a day off work on the day after the course. This will give you time to recover from the travel, as well as the course itself, and it will also give you the chance to work through your notes and adapt your personalised timetable whilst events are still fresh in your mind.

Options

There are more likely to be optional sessions during residential study schools, and often two sessions might be run at once, so you will have to make choices. These are best made in advance, if you have been able to obtain enough detailed information about the way the school is going to be run. You can always change your mind on the day, but it can be difficult to make what might be crucial decisions about which session to attend when you only have a few minutes over coffee to do this, or when you are asked to put your name down for sessions at the beginning of the school. You want to be free to focus your energy on the learning process, and managing these choices in advance will help with that process.

Unless you are told otherwise, always assume that residential study schools will be a compulsory part of your course; it may be that you cannot successfully complete the course until you have attended a residential school. They are always busy and tiring events, but they have all the advantages of day schools, with the added benefits that you will have the time to get to know more of your fellow students and spend time considering the wider implications of your study as well as simply taking in information. If you plan well, and focus throughout the weekend, you will find that the benefit of such schools will be felt within your studying tasks for several weeks, or even months, after the event.

Workshops

Workshops come in a variety of guises, from sessions run by your professional body as part of your continuing professional development structure, to evening sessions run by your course provider, to work-based projects forming part of your research tasks. They should not be confused with discussion groups, which might have a different focus for discussion each week and are often run by groups of students without tutorial help. Workshops will always run to a theme, with specific tasks to be covered and discussion taking place within this structure. They can be an essential part of your learning experience (particularly if you are taking a vocational distance and open learning course) or they can be run as non-essential backup for students who want additional support in one area of their studying. In the latter case, the workshops might not be specific to your subject area, but more general sessions on aspects of studying such as note taking, essay and report writing or presentation skills. In order to get the most out of them, there are several questions to ask before you commit to attending them.

Do I need this?

A basic question, but one that is not often asked. If a workshop session is regularly scheduled as an optional part of your course, you will have to evaluate (usually by attending the first session) how useful it will be to you, and consider whether the cost to you (in terms of travel costs and time) is worth it. This might seem like a negative approach to take, but whilst most workshop sessions will form a valuable and enjoyable part of your course, if you feel that you are not getting enough out of them, take action now to rectify the situation. You might simply choose not to attend, but if there are problems you can tackle (you need workshops that are more specific to your needs, you find members of the group unhelpful or overbearing, you find the timing inconvenient), then take a positive step by discussing these with the course provider before abandoning the idea altogether.

How will it impact upon my schedule?

It is common for distance and open learning students to see workshops as discreet entities in themselves, taking up no more space in their schedule than the hour or so it takes to attend them. In reality, they can take up many hours of your time, as you prepare for them, attend them and then work through the learning experience in order to incorporate what you have learnt into your overall course material. This is not a problem, it is a useful and productive way to work, but you do need to ensure that you have amended your personalised timetable to reflect the true time commitment that workshops will require of you.

Are there other opportunities linked to this workshop?

One of the most valuable aspects of workshops is the chance they offer for you to network with other students, tutors and professionals in your field. As you become more used to the workshop format, you can use the time, both during and after the workshop, to meet these potential supporters and increase your contact list. You might not meet these students again after just one workshop together, so you need to ensure that you can build on what you have learnt together by keeping in email contact after the event. If you can make contact with professionals in your field, you will also have the opportunity to discuss with them how your course might impact upon your career and any other courses you might want to attend in the future.

How can I prepare to make the most of it?
This will differ from workshop to workshop, but at the very least you will need to find out exactly what is involved in each session, what knowledge you will be expected to have and how the workshop will be structured. This might vary from a lecture with questions afterwards to a discussion session with minimal interference from the tutor. You might be asked to tackle practical problems relating to your research tasks or talk through complex theoretical issues. As with so much else, preparation will be vital if you are to use the experience to its full potential.

What might hamper my learning experience?
Several factors might hamper your ability to learn effectively, and these are usually to do with the format of the workshop session rather than its content. Workshops are designed to be highly interactive and relatively informal, which is a positive way to learn as long as you can cope with this. One overbearing member of the group can put you off, planning methods with which you are unfamiliar can confuse you, and loud, passionate discussions can be intimidating. None of these hurdles to effective learning is insurmountable, as long as you analyse the situation so that you can pinpoint the problem. The most effective way to counteract these problems is usually to work with the workshop group in advance, emailing members to confirm the ground you are about to cover and discussing the approaches you might take. In this way you will feel that you have contributed to the session, and benefited from it, even if on the day you are not the most vocal contributor.

How can I get involved?
If you want to become involved beyond contributing to the general discussion, or working through ideas and challenges ahead of the session, you might like to consider running a workshop session yourself. Although these sessions are supported by tutors or other professionals, there is often scope for students to run a session, perhaps giving a presentation to the group or leading the discussion. This might seem daunting, but it will help you within your learning process, as you will have to put your thoughts in order so you can express them to others. It also overcomes the problem of one member of the group taking over the event. It will help you to develop your presentation skills in a relatively relaxed atmosphere, which is always useful, especially if you are going to be asked to give a more formal, high-level presentation as part of the course assessment.

Workshop sessions offer you the chance to take control of your learning, interact with your fellow students and get a wider support base for the future. You may not attend all the workshops on offer, but you can ensure that you squeeze the maximum benefit from each one, which in itself will be a positive experience that goes beyond the content of the workshop, by allowing you to develop your research and learning skills in a supportive atmosphere.

Additional support sessions

These may not, strictly speaking, be part of your course structure, but they can be valuable experiences nevertheless. Many distance and open learning students feel frustrated when they discover, too late, additional learning opportunities that would have supported them in their course. Some of these are listed here, so you can find out if any of them might be available to you.

Other course lectures

One of the advantages to be gained from attending weekend or residential study sessions is that it gives you the chance to wander around a campus and see what is on offer. You might find courses that are similar to your own, and this may allow you to follow up your findings with a request to join lecture groups occasionally. If lectures are taking place that interest you, talk to your course providers to see whether it would be possible for you to sit in on them; they are not always strictly reserved for one set of students. If the lecturer does not object to you sitting in, this can be an easy way to supplement your distance and open learning course materials, and allows you to meet other students with similar interests and goals.

Postgraduate seminars

In a similar way, it is worth finding out whether there are any postgraduate groups on the campus who hold seminars or discussion groups in areas relevant to your studying. Again, you will have to work through your course providers to see whether it is possible for you to sit in on some of these sessions, which are often wide ranging and might offer you clues about new approaches.

Local interest groups

You might not already be a member of your local history society, for example, or your council planning committee, or a waterways action group, but any of these activities might supplement your studying by supporting the wider context in which you are learning. These groups can take up too much of your time, so joining them will need careful thought, but they could enrich your learning experience.

Study skills workshops

General study skills workshops are not confined to universities: local adult education centres run them, as do local further education colleges. Although you will want to check out what your course provider is offering before committing yourself to a course elsewhere, an evening class in presentation skills, for example, where you can practise your techniques away from your fellow distance and open learning students, can be an effective way to boost your confidence.

Information technology sessions

You should be offered help by your course provider, so that you can deal with any of the IT challenges your course puts in your way. However, wider IT skills (such as the proficient use of a data projector for presentations, or advanced searching on the internet) can be developed by enrolling in courses locally; even local schools sometimes now run night classes in IT.

Conference sessions

The issue of when and how to take part in conferences will be discussed in Chapter 6. It is worth mentioning here that conferences are not confined to academic circles. Your professional body will run conferences, as will other interest groups. Once you are on the emailing list for a variety of organisations you will hear about all sorts of conferences. You will usually decide whether or not to attend based upon the papers and presentations being given, but you also need to assess the value of less formal sessions outside the conference hall. These sessions may cover peripheral subjects less directly relevant to the conference theme, but which might be central to your research area.

Support from professional bodies

Even if your course is not entirely vocational, you might gain useful support from a professional body, who might offer help with planning your research, or give you information about further courses and conferences in which you might have an interest. Accessing their website would be the place to start: events and professional support systems are usually well publicised.

You will not have time to take part in every additional learning situation that might be available to you, but you are in a position to pick and choose which support sessions you attend as your course progresses. Setting aside time each month to consider new learning opportunities could make a difference not only to your studying achievements, but also to your whole view of your subject and the way in which you approach it. The table below will help you to visualise the components of your course and the ways in which you can maximise their benefit to you.

Course component	Key advantages	Management strategy
Hard copy packs	Allow you to see your course at a glance; you can work on them anywhere	Organise them as early as possible; return to them frequently
Videos, audio cassette tapes, DVDs	Allow you to work at a time that suits you; they can be viewed again	Make notes, label and file them, watch them with fellow students if possible
TV and radio broadcasts	Bring an immediacy to your learning experience	Tape them and make notes; reference and file each one
CD-ROMs	Can be interactive and contain vast amounts of easily accessible data	List your objectives before you access them; see them as just one of your tools
Independent e-learning	You can work at your own pace; you will develop your own study database	Get help when you need it; remain focused on your key task at all times
Guided e-learning	The material will be course-specific and easily accessible	Be critical of everything you read; use only the most helpful sites
Face-to-face tutorials	You can engage more fully with your tutor to gain advice on your course	Be prepared; maximise the time by writing out a plan in advance
Day schools	You will meet your fellow students and tutors in an informal setting	Prepare fully so as to make the most of the available time
Residential schools	Will crystallise many elements of your course	Be ready to ask questions, plan your schedule and network widely

(*continued*)

Course component	Key advantages	Management strategy
Workshops	An informal way to try out new ideas and approaches	Take the lead in arranging workshops if they do not already exist
Additional support sessions	Your engagement with them can be flexible and proactive	Evaluate the merit of these sessions at all stages of your course

Spot guide

The key points to remember from this chapter:

- take each course component in turn and decide how you can work most constructively with it
- whatever the teaching or learning method, try to keep your notes as uniform as possible
- mastering e-learning will be fundamental to your success: become familiar with it early in your course
- making the most of face-to-face learning relies on thorough preparation and your ability to take some control over the learning situation
- day schools can be frantic: know what you want before you arrive
- residential study schools are a vital opportunity within your studying: develop strategies for making the most of them
- workshops and discussion groups will be positive elements in your course as long as you can develop the most effective learning techniques for these situations

4 Managing your Course

Troubleshooting guide

Use this chapter for help if:

- you want to organise your course material before your workload increases
- you are anxious about the initial workload of studying
- you are not sure how to plan your studying throughout your course
- you need to develop time management strategies
- you feel that you might want to take a break from studying
- you need help in organising your studying, work and domestic lives more effectively
- you want to develop productive relationships with your lecturers, tutors, mentor and supervisor

▶ Before your course starts

How much work you *can do* in preparation for your course will depend upon your circumstances; how much work you *need to do* will depend on your course. If you do nothing at all, this need not be a problem, but if you can spend some time preparing and planning this will help you in four ways. Firstly, it will help to make your workload easier once the course has begun. Secondly, it will alert you to any potential hurdles you can overcome now, rather than when you are under more pressure. Thirdly, it will allow you to develop an overview of the course, what you are being asked to do and what is being offered to you – how far your studying and research might extend. This sense of knowing 'the bigger picture' will stay with you throughout your course and help you to remain focused. Lastly, carrying out any of the preparation suggested here will result in you feeling more in control of the course and the learning process: this will be vital in the management of your course.

You could, I am sure, produce your own lengthy list of things to do before your course begins. It is a good idea to make this list, rather than just have a vague mental note of what you might do. Not only is there the satisfaction of crossing items off the list, it is an easy way to raise your motivation as you begin your course. Here I have listed just a few ideas to help you to begin on your list:

- *Organise any course materials you have been sent*: as I mentioned in the last chapter, filing the materials you have been sent is the first step in managing your course. It will ensure that you are in control of the course even before you begin. It is a good idea to keep a miscellaneous section in the filing system, in which you can put material that is bothering you: instructions that are unclear to you, or course materials you had not expected and which may not fit into your initial plans. There is no need to worry unduly about these at this stage, but by filing them separately you will have them ready so you can query points with your tutor at the first opportunity.
- *Read through tutorial material*: again, this will help you to feel that you can master the overview of your course. This is not a detailed read, but more a process of 'dipping into' the course in its entirety, as was suggested in the last chapter.
- *Obtain a local library card*: an obvious point, but if your course provider is many miles from your home, you might need to arrange for a library card at your local university or college; your course provider will help you to do this.
- *Apply for an international NUS card*: you might join the National Union of Students as a standard part of your enrolment procedure (although not all providers can offer this facility for their students), but distance and open learning students often overlook the benefits (in particular, cheap travel and flights) of also applying for an international NUS card.
- *Begin to prepare your personalised timetable*: this will be examined in more detail later in this chapter. It will form the basis of your course management, and is most productively begun now, before pressure of work makes it difficult to find the time to work through it clearly and in detail.
- *Begin to produce reading and research notebooks*: as a backup to your personalised timetable, you might produce notebooks that record your reading and research to date and show you at a glance the reading and research tasks that are still outstanding. These will be explored in more detail in Chapter 5, but beginning on them early can help you to feel that

you are making the course your own, rather than having it imposed upon you.

- *Share your plans with your support groups*: once you are clear about the basic outline of your personalised study timetable, you will be ready to share it with your family, friends and work colleagues. I am not suggesting that you offer your work colleagues a copy, but you could let them know when key tasks are likely to fall so that you can begin to make plans now, if you need to, to lighten your workload at some points during the course.
- *Decide upon your ideal learning outcomes*: there is a lot of theoretical jargon used nowadays to describe learning outcomes and learning processes and these can be disquieting for the less experienced student. Essentially, learning outcomes are simply the end products that you can expect from your course, and they will range from increasing your general skills base (getting better at presenting your ideas, for example) to specific gains such as mastering an aspect of your subject and gaining a qualification. Learning outcomes will be incorporated into the design of your course, but it is far better for you if this process is based on a dialogue. Time spent now working through what it is you want to achieve by the end of the course will allow you to be an active rather than a passive distance and open learner, and will give you the chance to talk to your tutors about what you would like the course to do for you, rather than just what you are expected to do for it.

Once you have made an assessment of the learning outcomes that you might expect to achieve from your course, you will be in a good position to feed these into your skills development plan, which is considered in detail in Chapter 6. This is not an isolated process: skills targets reflect learning outcomes and can be evaluated as part of your overall course management. This is how it works in practice.

assess your skills base

↓

produce a skills inventory

↓

target key skills for improvement

(continued)

↓

consider how the stated learning outcomes of your course will feed into your skills development plan

↓

analyse whether you can develop your own learning outcomes within the course to enhance your skills development plan

↓

work through your plan of action

↓

reassess your skills development plan

↓

where are you now in terms of your personal skills action plan?

↓

where are you now in terms of your course learning outcomes?

↓

rework your skills development plan so that you can move on to your next area of development

By incorporating this process into your distance and open learning experience you can ensure that you meet the targets of your course, but also that the course learning outcomes are relevant to your personal skills development plan. You will remain on target for the learning outcomes of your course and be in control of your own skills development. Another advantage of this process is that it allows you to work productively with your course tutors in a defined and recognisable way. They are interested in the learning outcomes that have informed their development of the course; you are also now interested in learning outcomes, and are aware that their learning outcomes will feed into your skills development in a positive way.

▶ The initial workload

It is easy to get the wrong impression about your course in the first few weeks. Your initial enthusiasm will carry you through, but you may suspect that you cannot keep up this work rate indefinitely, and if you ease up the course will overwhelm you. This is not usually a case of working harder, just of working smarter, and there are several ways in which you can do this.

Refer back to your personalised timetable

Your personalised timetable is going to be vital in the early stages of your course. When you begin to feel as if the work is never-ending, you will be able to refer to it and be reassured that you have a set number of tasks to complete in a week and, once these are accomplished, you can then take some well-earned rest. By using your timetable in this way you will not let any contact with other students put you off. There is always someone who seems to be doing more than anyone else (although this is not usually the case in reality) but your timetable will keep you on track, knowing that you are doing enough work to succeed on your course.

Gauge your work rate

We tend not to analyse how we work through each of our study tasks, and this is particularly true of those students who are doing paid work as they study. Within our jobs, much of what we do is second nature; we use techniques and short cuts that we have developed over time and we tend not to think too hard about our efficiency, it comes naturally. When you begin your course, you will be asked to carry out less familiar activities: producing assignments, critiquing established research, preparing presentations and working through reading lists and research tasks. If you are working to schedule you may not be concerned with how efficiently you are undertaking these tasks, but if you feel that there is simply too much work to do, it is worth checking your work rate. How many pages of a textbook can you work through, making notes, in an hour? Is this more than you could do last week? Do you do it more swiftly in the evenings, in the day or at weekends? By thinking of your studying in this analytical way you can begin to find the optimum time and method for the tasks ahead of you, and hopefully reassure yourself that you are speeding up in the basics of your course.

Analyse each type of task

We all find some aspects of the learning process easier than others, and now is the time to analyse your strengths and weaknesses. There is usually a way to improve your output. If, for example, you find note taking from books difficult, work out why. Do you stray from the chapters that you intended to study? Do you read and reread sentences to try to fathom their meaning? Do you write reams of notes that are almost as dense as the book itself? If you do any of these things, then take a break and rearrange your work mode. It may be better for you to photocopy the portion of the book you need (keeping within the copyright regulations posted in your library) and then highlight the relevant sections, reducing these sections to key notes on cards rather than full notes. If you tire easily with this type of close work, you might benefit from working to a new routine, such as making notes on six pages of text and then taking a break from it to do other tasks for half an hour. It is only when you analyse each task, particularly any you suspect are taking a disproportionate amount of time, that you can begin to work in a more efficient way.

Become familiar with the work

You are not going to become the ideal distance and open learner overnight, and this is not a continual test of your ability to work at your most efficient at all times. If you can accept that it is going to take several weeks to become familiar with new ways of working and the unfamiliar challenges you are now facing, you will reduce the pressure you are putting on yourself a great deal. This is more important than it might seem at first glance. Too many distance and open learners feel that they are failing, and so lose motivation and the incentive to manage a course which they feel has already beaten them, when in reality they are improving all the time and are working well within the confines and time restraints of the course. Give yourself the time to make a few initial mistakes, to become more fluent in the way you work: it will become second nature to you in time, and there is no need to waste your energy and lose focus by worrying unnecessarily at this early stage.

Tame your reading lists

Reading lists can be the bane of many students' lives, whether they are taking a distance and open learning course or not. They are usually given out with too little indication of how they are to be used, and they are often also either too scant to help you through every eventuality, or so long that you feel as if you could never wade through them in the time available. All graduates could tell you of the books that they fully intended to read but never quite managed to open; the trick is to be ruthless and ask questions. If the list is huge, are you really expected to read every book? Are there some books that are more relevant to your research and learning aims? If the list is scant, can your tutor suggest, at this early stage in the course, supplementary reading to boost the list? If the books all seem too advanced, do not let embarrassment get in the way: ask for details of a more basic guide, just to get you going. Once you have asked these questions, and tailored your list to suit your needs, Chapter 5 will help you to use your reading time effectively.

Take an overview of your tasks and course structure

It is difficult, when you are embroiled in several tasks at once, each of which seems vital, to take a more detached overview of what you are doing, yet this is essential if you are to reduce the pressure. If you know that you have a certain number of tasks to do in a weekend, for example, you will be able to switch effortlessly from one task to another if you find your energy levels lowering. This will prevent you from wading through a book at a snail's pace when, if you left it alone for an hour to carry out other study tasks, you would do both tasks more efficiently. Having a clear picture of this section of your course structure in your mind (this weekend's work will get me a third of the way through this assignment, for example) will keep you motivated. Taking five minutes off to remind yourself of this will never be time wasted.

Prioritise your workload

In an ideal world you would be able to complete all your tasks within the time frame you have set yourself, and for much of your course this will be the case. However, as things do not always work out as we planned, your personalised timetable will indicate to you which tasks are essential in each study period, and which can be shifted to another time slot if necessary. You will be forced to do this in any case if you find a particular task more onerous or time-consuming than you had expected, but doing it within the structure of your personalised timetable will give you the confidence and flexibility to move tasks around without feeling that you are letting yourself down.

Stick to your minimum requirements

Some periods of studying are going to be harder than others, and there will inevitably be times when you just have to work for more hours than you had expected. This is not a bad thing: we all know the pleasure of working really hard and then achieving a goal in the early hours of the morning. If you find yourself in this position, especially in the initial stages of your course, you will know that you have taken the option of moving some tasks within your timetable, you are working to your best rate of efficiency at this stage, and you will not have to work this hard for more than a few days before you can return to a more manageable working pattern. Beyond this, stick with your tasks until you have completed what your timetable shows you is the minimum requirement for that period of study. It is better to do this and then rearrange your timetable for the future, than leaving essential tasks to one side, only to find that you are genuinely behind and with a reduced scope to reorganise your timetable.

Take time off

This may sound like contradictory advice, having just reminded you that some periods of study are going to be hard work, perhaps more demanding than you had expected. However, if you simply continue to work with maximum effort during each spare minute of the day, you will soon be working less effectively. You need time to wind down and replenish your energy, and your family needs to see you sometimes! Our brains are not very good at simply taking in masses of information with no time to process the implications of the data, so taking time off, within the structure of your personalised timetable, is actually just another way of working. As you take some rest, your brain will be processing information. You will soon find that the answer to a research problem comes to you in the shower, or you wake up with the perfect opening sentence for your assignment ready formed in your mind. Regular time off is essential: it is not a waste of your time, it is just a different way of allowing your brain to work.

The structure of your course

Having suggested that you take regular time off from your immediate and regular study tasks, it is also a sensible idea to work out whether you will need to take a more prolonged break during your course. If you are taking regular short breaks, there may be no need for you to consider a more extended break, although your professional or home life might dictate this. If you take an overview of the structure of your course, once you have encapsulated it within your personalised study timetable, you will be able to see obvious points at which you might be able to take a break, but it is more usually a case of being able to identify those points at which you can take the pressure off yourself a little. If your timetable is no more than a solid itinerary of hard work for the duration of the course, its effectiveness as a management tool is greatly reduced. Instead, you will need to identify those weeks that are easier than others, and try to work within this pattern, not only so that your work, social and home lives do not suffer disproportionately because of your course, but also so that you have some leeway when it comes to reworking the timetable in order to accommodate tasks you have yet to complete. There are fundamental guidelines to follow here if you are to maximise the value of your timetable and make your learning process as efficient, and enjoyable, as possible:

- *Produce a personalised timetable as early as possible*: although you will not be in a position to make a definitive personalised timetable in the first week or so of your course, it makes sense to begin the task as early as possible, preferably before your course begins, as soon as you receive the course information. You will be regularly updating and amending the timetable, but if you begin early it will act as an anchor to your thoughts and tasks from the earliest stages: you will feel in control from the very beginning.
- *Analyse the tasks to be included*: later in this chapter the personalised study timetable will be discussed in more detail, with an example for you to work from, but it is worth noting here that each task to be included can be categorised, so that you balance your tasks each week. A task might, for example, be essentially a reading task, research or writing up. In addition, it might be designated as 'hard', 'moderate' or 'easy' or as 'quick' or 'time-consuming'. By designating each task in this way before you put it into your personalised timetable, you can be sure that you are not overburdening yourself in any week, and can guarantee that you are giving yourself a range of tasks, so you can add variety to your workload.
- *Include family and work commitments*: it has already been suggested that your personalised timetable is the place to start when trying to dovetail your work, home and study commitments. However, this is essentially your tool for study, so only the most pressing or time-consuming events should be included, such as family holidays and major work events.
- *Define each week according to its workload*: in the same way that you will have different types of task, some more vital than others, so too will you be able to take an overview of your course workload by considering the nature of each week, as it is now shown in your personalised timetable. It is useful to mark up weeks as 'light weeks', 'hard weeks', 'reading weeks' and so on. In this way you can easily keep in mind the pattern of your studying.
- *Always remember to include new tasks as they arise*: this is a positive move, because it ensures that you feel comfortable with your study workload and in control of the learning process. When students are

given a new task, particularly if it is unforeseen, the most common reaction is a groan of disbelief that they are being be handed yet more work. Once you have a personalised timetable, your reaction will be quite different: you can immediately plan where the task will most sensibly fit into your timetable. Rather than wasting time worrying about your workload, you will remain in control and getting on with the work in hand.

- *Rework your timetable regularly*: as well as including new tasks in your timetable, and deleting other tasks that have become unnecessary (this will happen!), you will also need to take the time every week or so to review the timetable. This will simply involve checking that everything is still working according to plan, you have not inadvertently completed a task set for next week (this will happen too!) and you are still happy with the overall pattern of the timetable for the next few weeks. This is one of the most enjoyable tasks ahead of you: it reminds you how much you have achieved (something entirely lacking for some students) and reassures you that the challenge ahead of you is manageable.

Time management

You already have time management skills, as you work through your daily routine and meet deadlines. The temptation with a distance and open learning course is that you can see it as entirely different from 'normal' life, something that must be bolted on to your existing schedule, a challenge that will differ in all aspects from everything you currently do. This is not the case, and imposing some structure on your studying is the first step towards being able to visualise your course as an extension of your life, rather than divorced from it. Distance and open learners face a greater challenge than full-time, on-site students because they need to develop high levels of self-discipline and maintain a study structure, but you can help yourself in this by answering the following questions.

Can you multitask?

The answer to this is clearly 'yes'. We multitask all the time, without giving it any great consideration. The question with distance and open learning is whether you can reasonably multitask within your studying, and it is a decision you need to make early on. If you are naturally good at highlighting textbooks whilst watching television, safe in the knowledge that you will be able to make watertight revision cards later, then there will be no problem with working in this way. If you can happily listen to a radio broadcast to gain an overview of it whilst planning an assignment, before listening to it again and making notes, you will do this. However, if you find even the most minor distraction ruins your concentration, then there is no point in multitasking more than you absolutely have to. If you spend hours searching the internet for a reference whilst trying to plan an essay and talking on the telephone, you could end up feeling exhausted, having achieved very little. Try multitasking at the outset of your course and work out as quickly as possible what works for you, then stick to your best working method.

Can you reuse experiences?

There is no need to reinvent the wheel simply because you are studying formally on a distance and open learning course. If you have given a presentation in the past, for example, write out your strengths and weaknesses as a presenter and only spend time working on the weaknesses: your strengths will come back to you naturally when you begin to rehearse. If you have carried out research in a field related to your course (perhaps a marketing survey or analysis of relevant research), then work through this first, to see if it can be adapted, rather than assuming that you have to begin again from scratch.

Have you finished a task?

It is not unusual for distance and open learning students to feel that their study tasks are never-ending. To some extent the tasks are never-ending: you could read for the rest of the year and still not have covered every piece of research that has been written up in your field. The secret is to know, categorically, when a task is complete, and so dispel the nagging feeling that you may be leaving something out, always getting behind. Once you accept that you *are* always leaving something out, that you can do no more than is necessary for each task to be accomplished, then you will relax with your studying. Set yourself tasks that are well defined within your personalised timetable, and work through each of them before resolutely moving on to the next task.

Where are the gaps?

We all have gaps in our days, and some of these are fundamental to our wellbeing. Whereas some people cannot conceive of foregoing their lunch hour, others cannot remember the last time they had one: both these categories of people have worked out the best system for them. No distance and open learning course is going to demand that you give up all your free time to study, but you can analyse your routine to see if there are any pockets of wasted time which can be converted to potential study time. Sitting on a train without a study text may be counterproductive, one less television programme a day might give you half a day more each week in which to study. Once you have found these pockets of time, they seem obvious, but for most of us the process of analysing our week in this way is necessary if we are to identify these time management opportunities. You have to strike a balance, there is no point in feeling as if you are either working or studying during every minute of every day, but filling up wasted time with tasks is a habit that is easy to develop, allowing you to keep on target without too great a sacrifice.

When and how do you work best?

I have already stressed the need to establish at which time of day you work best, but now you also need to analyse how you work best. This might be in a methodical way, allocating time each day to studying, or in a more sporadic way, working in bursts of several hours a few times a week. Do not assume that there is a 'best' way of working: there is not, it is up to you to decide how you can be most productive and work this approach into your personalised timetable.

How is your skills base developing?

There can be a tendency for distance and open learners to presume that any studying is a good thing, but this is not necessarily the case, particularly when you have a whole series of tasks to fit into your week. Within your personalised timetable you will be including tasks that help you to develop and broaden your skills base, but this is not an open-ended task. If you have booked onto a study skills course on effective note taking, for example, you need only attend as long as you find it useful. If you feel after the first session that, after all, you do have the essential skills needed to carry you forward, it is better to move on to your next area of skill development, rather than spending your time completing a course that is of limited value to you. As long as the tutor knows that this has been a considered decision, leaving a course early in this way will not prevent you from returning to it at a later date if you feel that your needs have changed.

Would feedback help?

Time management cannot be undertaken effectively in a vacuum. A student with years of experience in distance and open learning courses would be able to produce and maintain a personalised timetable with confidence, but most of us need some feedback along the way. You will be aware if things begin to go wrong, if you are getting behind with your schedule, and your tutor can help you to get back on track. There is, however, a danger that, if things are going very well, you will simply load more and more tasks into your timetable and so end up with an unreasonable amount of work to do. If you take your personalised timetable with you to your sessions with a tutor (or email it to your tutor as part of your ongoing assessment), you will find that your tutor is in the best position to help you to balance your timetable according to your circumstances and the requirements of your course. This role need not be confined to your tutor. Your family and work colleagues can also help if you explain to them how you intend the timetable to work. None of us has the definitive answer to time management, you will always look back and see ways in which you might have done things better, but if you talk through your timetable with others, you may be pleasantly surprised at how many creative working and studying ideas there are around you, ideas that can be incorporated into your study routine so that you can study in the most enjoyable and productive way.

▶ Taking a break

I hope by now that you are convinced of the need to take a short break from your studying from time to time. Here I want to look at the possibility that, at some point, you might need to take a more extended break from your course. This is perhaps the most common reason for students simply dropping out of distance and open learning courses; they feel that they need a break, are not sure how to go about it and so abandon the course altogether rather than working methodically through their needs and assessing the best way to move forward.

Be clear about your needs

All students feel, at one time or another, that they cannot meet all the demands being placed upon them. When you come to consider it, this is an inherent part of any course: each tutor makes demands, each module has deadlines and you also have a life to fit around the course. In most instances, this results in little more than a rather more pressurised period of study that leads to a sense of achievement and relief once it is over. In some cases, however, the feeling goes beyond what you might normally expect. You begin to feel that you will never catch up and, as importantly, you stop enjoying what should be a satisfying and interesting challenge.

Use your timetable to plan your break

One of the noticeable features of students who take an unplanned break is that they struggle to resume their studying, not because they have any less talent, or energy, but just because they have not planned their break carefully. Once you have decided that a break has become necessary, work with your personalised timetable to ascertain at which point a break most naturally falls (after the completion of an assignment, for example). Although this may delay your plans by a few weeks, it will ensure that you return to studying with a clear-cut break behind you and a well-defined set of tasks in front of you.

Talk to your tutor

One of the advantages of planning your break in this methodical way is the positive approach you can take to your decision. You can then talk it through with your tutor in a constructive way, sure that you will be supported as you move through this period in your studying life. Talking things through with your tutor is essential, even if your course is open-ended and the timing is left to the student. Although in this case you could take an unannounced break and not suffer in your overall results, your tutor will be left wondering why you have not been in touch, and you will be left dreading your emails in case they are from your course provider about new study tasks. Once you have made your decision known in this way, you will be relieved of any pressure, ensuring that your study break really is a rest. The other benefit of talking things through with your tutor is that he or she will have seen this situation before and so will have useful tips about how to make a break effective.

Be realistic about the length of break you need

The suggestions above are designed to help you to see your break for what it is: a sensible and reasoned response to circumstances, rather than a failure. If you feel guilty about taking a break, suspecting that you have failed in some way, you are likely to be unrealistic about how long you need to take away from studying. Your efforts to please by taking the shortest possible break would be misdirected: your tutors are only concerned that you return to your studying at a time that suits you so that you achieve the best possible result in the end. Planning the timing of a break can be difficult, but err on the side of caution. Talk through the situation with your family, friends, work colleagues and tutor, decide upon the length of time you think you need, and then add a few weeks to it. It is better to give yourself time to reintroduce yourself to the course materials and the workload rather than rushing back in before you are ready.

Resume your studying in an organised way

Once your break is over there will be a temptation to throw yourself back into the work in a piecemeal fashion, hoping that your enthusiasm will get you back up to speed. The enthusiasm is clearly a good sign, and one that you will want to capitalise on, so make sure that you have worked out a totally reviewed and revised personalised timetable, taking account of any changes that have been made in the course structure during your absence. It will also help if you wean yourself back into work by spending the first week on lighter tasks, such as general reading, reviewing your reading and research notebooks and catching up with your email networking lists. After this short space of time you will be ready to resume your studying in the most effective way, sure that you have not missed anything vital and your mind is again fully engaged with the studying that is ahead of you.

Maximise the benefits of your break

Time passes quickly when you are studying, particularly if you are combining other work with your course: it passes even more quickly when you are taking a break from studying. If you are planning a break because you feel exhausted and unable to cope with the demands of your course for a time, you would be well advised to take a complete break from all aspects of your course. However, it is more common for distance and open learning students to need time just to catch their breath, reassess where they are in the studying process and plan their time more effectively, or tackle pressing work or home demands. In the latter case, a little studying is usually a good thing. It keeps you in touch with your course, reducing the effort required to work your way back into it, and it allows you to catch up on old tasks that have been left languishing at the bottom of your personalised timetable. You will, of course, have to be alert to the possibility of working too hard (this is meant to be a break), but if you plan well, limiting yourself to 'light' tasks and giving yourself plenty of time to complete them, you might find this approach more beneficial than leaving aside your learning altogether.

Consider taking a break between courses

Despite the fact that some distance and open learners feel the need to take a break sometimes, it would be inaccurate to suggest that distance and open learning courses are in themselves the problem. They are carefully designed to be as flexible and satisfying as possible, and the reason they are so successful as a teaching and learning method is that students enjoy them. This can lead inevitably to students moving straight from one course onto another, developing their skills and enhancing their qualifications at every stage. This is always a positive move, but you might like to think about whether you should take a break (perhaps of just a few weeks) between courses. This will allow you to catch up on your 'normal' life, and give you the chance to work through some of the points in Chapter 1 as you go about choosing your next course. This will ensure that you choose the best course for your learning methods and your developing academic and professional needs, so you can begin each course with renewed energy and confidence that it is the right course for you.

Your personalised timetable

A personalised timetable is the best way to incorporate your studying and learning processes into the rest of your life. It will help you to maximise your learning opportunities and minimise the potential problems you might face as your course progresses. It is never a static document, but rather a tool to be used: you will often add tasks to it, and you will regularly review it to monitor your progress and amend your schedule. At the outset of the course it will be a skeleton timetable, including only those tasks that are obvious to you from your initial course literature and skills inventory. As time moves on it will become more complex, but it should always be kept within manageable parameters. It is *not* simply a list of tasks that have to be completed whatever the cost to you; instead it is a way of managing your time and keeping a productive balance between varying study tasks and assessment challenges.

The way in which you structure your personalised timetable will depend upon the type of course that you are undertaking, but there are several basic guidelines to follow, whatever the nature of your course.

Monitor your workload

A year or so of solid work, with no variation in workload and no let up in the pressure you are working under, is never going to be a productive way of learning. Your personalised timetable is there to set personal restraints, to ensure that you are managing your workload rather than letting it manage you. It is only by viewing the overall structure of your course in this way that you can reasonably expect to give yourself some less pressurised time within your studying, which will keep you motivated when the pressure is more intense. It is also the most effective way to monitor your progress in your learning methods and vary the style of learning you adopt. Tasks that may have taken many hours in the first weeks of your course will become routine and far less time-consuming as your learning methods improve, and this change will be satisfyingly reflected in your personalised timetable.

Add variety to your tasks

It is not easy for any of us to work unremittingly at one type of task for hours on end without any break in the routine or variation in the type of task being undertaken. It is not always clear to distance and open learners that there are other ways to work, given that they have tasks which have to be completed in a certain space of time and they are, for much of the time, working alone. For students on a full contact course this variation is offered to them automatically. During an average study day they might be expected to spend some time in the library, an hour or so in lectures and a further hour in a seminar. They are likely to spend time discussing the course (and life in general) with their fellow students, and will feel happy about planning their next assignment in a relatively relaxed way, jotting down ideas over several days before working on a full and detailed plan. When asked to spend all day in the library (when they are approaching their examinations, for example) they often find this incredibly difficult and their work rate dips as a result. For the distance and open learner, sitting and working alone at one task for many hours is a common experience, but not necessarily the best way forward. I have already suggested that you need to monitor your work rate so as to maintain your efficiency, and a personalised timetable allows you to do this. Rather than wasting time (and losing the flow of your thoughts) by considering what additional task to do in order to break up your current task, you will already have the task in place, waiting for your attention.

Revise your schedule frequently

Personalised timetables are perhaps the most fun at the outset. You can enjoy spending an hour or so working through the initial itinerary you have received and deciding how to spread the tasks over the duration of the course. Your personalised timetable looks perfect, you feel organised and in control, and the temptation is then to avoid adding to it at all, in case you ruin your perfect plan. You must overcome this temptation: a personalised timetable only works well if you are prepared to return to it on a weekly basis so that you can make alterations and update it. You will not want to waste too long on this planning task, but it is essential that you keep doing it regularly; once your personalised timetable is out of date, not only is it valueless as a tool, it can lead you to underestimate (or overestimate) the workload you are facing, with disastrous results.

Adapt your timetable and work rate

Distance and open learning students are highly motivated, which is why the results of such courses are so impressive. You will already be aware that there will be times when you have to draw upon that motivation to work harder than you had expected, and this will not cause you any undue problems. However, if you find that this more intense work rate continues over a period of weeks, analyse your personalised timetable before you assume that the course is beyond you. It is far more likely that you have simply mismanaged your personalised timetable, giving yourself too much work in some weeks and not enough in others, or that you did not adequately revise the schedule when a new assignment was unexpectedly handed to you. Working too hard and in a fog of confusion is unsustainable in the long term; a little judicious alteration to your personalised timetable can alleviate the stress without compromising your overall results.

Share your timetable

If your personalised timetable is to be an effective management tool, it must be shared with your family, work colleagues and tutor. Most of the alterations you make will affect nobody but yourself, and so can simply be incorporated into the timetable as a routine part of your study time, but remember that your family will also be relying upon the timetable, looking forward to the 'light' weeks when you can catch up on your family commitments, so make sure that everyone is aware of any major changes you have decided to make to it.

The following example reflects the personalised timetable of a distance and open learning student who is several weeks into a professional development course in human resources, aware of both the immediate tasks to be tackled and the long-term goals to be reached. It is captured here in a moment in time: in reality it would have changed within a week or so as new circumstances dictate changes. I have assumed a ten-week section of a course: you may prefer to complete a personalised timetable for the whole of your course, but it is usually more easily handled in stages like this, allowing you to review your progress at the end of the ten-week period and produce a new personalised timetable at that point, incorporating any incomplete tasks and introducing new goals. Note that the time has been divided, as was suggested in Chapter 2, into 'regular', 'wish' and 'extra' time.

Week one (heavy week)

Regular	prepare for day school in week three • check accommodation • decide on sessions to attend • contacts list? read Hensley, MacDonald and Jenks texts and make notes three video clips to view – with Mike? complete tutor pack 1
Wish	work through reading list from module B, revise reading notebook check research notebook for assignment on recruitment in IT review video clip notes and check on further programmes
Extra	contact career development workshop group on email to arrange discussion session at day school

Week two (light week)

Regular	work through self-assessment test six – recap on five? attend presentation skills workshop #1 prepare visual aids for presentation – for everyone?
Wish	
Extra	library visit for research on recruitment assignment

Week three (light week)

Regular	DAY SCHOOL attend presentation skills workshop #2
Wish	complete plan for recruitment assignment
Extra	last-minute rehearsals for group presentation – contact the group

Week four (heavy week)

Regular	attend presentation skills workshop #3? give group presentation write up recruitment assignment report begin assignment on graduate training programmes complete tutor pack 2
Wish	develop reading and research sheets for dissertation
Extra	

Week five (reading week)

Regular	revise and update reading notebook book time on the CD-ROM at library work on graduate training programmes essay complete tutor pack 3 (work-based project preparation)
Wish	
Extra	reading and research lists for dissertation done?

(*continued*)

Week six (supervision week)

Regular	see supervisor re dissertation planning – review plan? review personalised timetable for supervisor session complete graduate training programmes essay, including bibliography view broadcast on entrepreneurs in Italy – useful for international essay in module D?
Wish	background reading for work-based project sit in on recruitment committee meeting?
Extra	

Week seven (planning week)

Regular	plan work-based project – discuss with manager complete tutor pack 4
Wish	check if I can lead workshop at residential school?
Extra	get updated health and safety form for work-based project

Week eight (reading week)

Regular	make notes on counselling theory texts
Wish	prepare for workshop at study school? review tutor packs – anything else to do? update reading notebook from module C reading list work through dissertation plan with Mike?
Extra	last-minute plans for work-based study?

Week nine (study school week)

Regular	RESIDENTIAL STUDY SCHOOL tutorial on graduate training programmes essay – make notes to prepare for it
Wish	revision cards for module B
Extra	website study chat room – Friday

Week Ten (planning week)

Regular	re-enrol on counselling skills course begin work-based study work out new personalised timetable
Wish	time out at home update reading and research notebooks
Extra	

Of course, your personalised timetable will differ from this in the detail, but there are some principles you can follow if you are to keep on track, with the least chance of either overwork or boredom slowing down your progress:

- Stick rigorously to your regular tasks, but vary them within your timetable
- See your wish tasks as a challenge each week – can you complete them?
- Extra tasks cannot be ignored; they must either be completed or abandoned, if you feel that you have been putting them off because they are not as important as you once thought
- Adapt your personalised timetable regularly, remembering to move unfinished tasks onto another week (not necessarily the following week)
- Remember that this is *your* personalised timetable. The tasks set by your course provider will fit relatively easily into the time available, so you will have plenty of space left to manage your own learning objectives.

In order to see how these principles work in practice, and how you might be able to adapt this personalised timetable to suit your own needs, each week is examined here to assess how the schedule was created.

Week one

Regular prepare for day school in week three
- check accommodation
- decide on sessions to attend
- contacts list?

read Hensley, MacDonald and Jenks texts and make notes
three video clips to view – with Mike?
complete tutor pack 1

Wish work through reading list from module B, revise reading notebook
check research notebook for assignment on recruitment in IT
review video clip notes and check on further programmes

Extra contact career development workshop group on email to arrange discussion session at day school

This is a busy week, probably because our student has had to carry over some tasks from her last personalised timetable. It is sometimes a good idea to give yourself an unstructured week between timetables so that you can catch up on incomplete tasks, if you feel that there is enough flexibility within your course structure to do this.

Note how she has varied her regular tasks, which include some solitary reading and note taking, some work on the first tutor pack for this section of the course (potentially a more dynamic, if still solitary, activity) and some work with her colleague Mike, who is her regular study partner. Her wish tasks are there as a confidence boost: they all need to be done at some point, but none of them will take long, so they will soon be ticked off her list. Her extra task is more of a problem: it should have been done some time ago, but she did not have the time, so this is her reminder to tackle the issue. Is she going to make contact and go ahead with arranging the disuc-sssion group, or has she been putting it off because she doubts its value, feeling that she could spend her time at the day school in a more productive way? By placing it in her extra tasks section she knows that she will have to make a decision this week.

Week two

Regular	work through self-assessment test six – recap on five?
	attend presentation skills workshop #1
	prepare visual aids for presentation – for everyone?
Wish	
Extra	library visit for research on recruitment assignment

Last week our student had a heavy workload: this week is more relaxed. The only pressure here is from her visit to the library, which she has been meaning to do for some time. Until she carries out this basic research she will not have grasped the range of material that she is likely to have to cover in the assignment, and so cannot make the plan for the assignment that she intends to produce next week. Beyond this, the week's regular tasks should not present a problem, as the self-assessment test is on the internet and can be accessed at any time; she does not anticipate that it will take her longer than an hour or so to complete it. The group presentation she is giving in week four has already been researched and her notes written up on prompt cards. She has already rehearsed her section and the visual aids will not take long to produce, even if she has to produce them for the whole group in order to ensure that they are uniform in layout.

There is another reason why this week is light on workload: she knows that this will give her the motivation to work really hard in week one, so as to keep week two as easy as possible. She is also aware that her work and family commitments might suffer in week one, so this week there will be a chance to catch up.

Week three

Regular DAY SCHOOL
attend presentation skills workshop #2
Wish complete plan for recruitment assignment
Extra last-minute rehearsals for group presentation – contact the group

Having worked alone for much of the first two weeks, our student is looking forward to a week in which she can gain information in an easier way and learn in a more social atmosphere. She prepared for the day school several weeks ago, and the presentation skills workshop merely requires her to turn up and work on the night, so this appears to be an easy week, particularly if the last-minute rehearsal with her presentation group can be fitted in after her presentations workshop. During this week, she will be adding significantly to her skills base.

Aware that this week's tasks might fit into a couple of days, she is happy to include planning her next assignment in her personalised timetable here, but will not be disappointed if she has to move it to the next week if things get more hectic than she had planned.

Week four

Regular attend presentation skills workshop #3?
give group presentation
write up recruitment assignment report
begin assignment on graduate training programmes
complete tutor pack 2
Wish develop reading and research sheets for dissertation
Extra

There are no extra tasks this week (unless she has had to add more in her regular review of her personalised timetable), but this is just as well, as her regular tasks are demanding. She is aware that she might be able to miss the final presentations workshop as it is dealing with aspects of presentations that do not yet concern her and the workshops are run several times a year. Her group presentation is her most important task this week, but she also has to write a report and begin to write a further major assignment. If she is to complete her tutor packs within the time she originally set for herself, she must work through tutor pack 2 this week.

Although this week is going to be busy, she has no extra tasks included in her schedule and beginning to prepare for her dissertation plan is not too pressing yet: she has two weeks to go until she has to meet with her supervisor.

Week five

Regular revise and update reading notebook
book time on the CD-ROM at library
work on graduate training programmes essay
complete tutor pack 3 (work-based project preparation)

Wish

Extra reading and research lists for dissertation done?

A solitary study week halfway through her ten-week personalised timetable, and one that will ensure that our student feels fully up to date with her course. So far she has had to produce a report, work on a major assignment and give a group presentation, as well as attending a demanding day school. Now is a good time for her to take stock, work through her study material and revise her reading and research notebooks. The only task beyond this is her extra task of producing reading and research lists for her dissertation. She knows that these must be completed by the end of this week, but hopes to have produced them in week four, so that this week is much more about taking in information than reproducing it. By the end of this week she will have done more than just tick off the tasks on her personalised timetable: she will feel fully in control of her course as a whole.

Week six

Regular see supervisor re dissertation planning – review plan?
review personalised timetable for supervisor session
complete graduate training programmes essay, including bibliography
view broadcast on entrepreneurs in Italy – useful for international essay in module D?

Wish background reading for work-based project
sit in on recruitment committee meeting?

Extra

There are no extra tasks this week, which will allow our student to focus on her meeting with her supervisor. Unlike a normal meeting with a tutor, this session has been set aside, at her request, to allow for disucsssion of her dissertation, an extended piece of research that is not due to be written for several months, but which she feels she needs to begin working towards now.

There are tasks to complete in addition to this meeting, such as background reading, completing an essay and viewing a broadcast, and these will combine to make this a heavy week of studying. Aware of this, our student has questioned whether she really has time to sit on the recruitment committee meeting that is held regularly by her employers. She is not a member of the committee, but asked to be allowed to sit in on meetings occasionally, so as to increase her understating of how recruitment policy decisions are made. She would like to be there, but is conscious of a number of pressing tasks this week, and knows that missing one meeting is not going to present a problem in the long term.

Week seven

Regular plan work-based project – discuss with manager
complete tutor pack 4
Wish check if I can lead workshop at residential school?
Extra get updated health and safety form for work-based project

Now that she has worked through so much of her planned studying, our student feels ready to branch out by offering to lead a workshop at the residential school to be held in week nine, but she has placed this in her wish task section, in case she loses her nerve at the last moment. She knows that the preparation will not take long, as she can lead a workshop on graduate training programmes. She has already produced her assignment on this and has plenty of 'spare' research material she can use during the session. If she does lead the workshop, she will be continuing to develop her presentation skills, which was one of her goals for this section of her studying.

Much of her focus this week will be on her workplace, as she has a busy schedule there, so she has incorporated work-based studying tasks within this week, such as discussing her project with her manager and ensuring that she has completed all the forms necessary to go ahead with the project. Tutor pack 4 is also a work-based learning pack, so her studying should dovetail well with her paid work during this week, and she is not anticipating any difficulties in completing the week's tasks on time.

Week eight

Regular make notes on counselling theory texts
Wish prepare for workshop at study school?
review tutor packs – anything else to do?
update reading notebook from module C reading list
work through dissertation plan with Mike?
Extra last-minute plans for work-based study?

This is an unusual week. Our student is uncertain as to how long the note taking on counselling theories might take (several students have suggested that it is a huge task) and she is concerned about a report she has to produce for her manager by the end of the week. So as to reduce her stress levels, but not waste time that could be productively incorporated into her personalised timetable, she has chosen to place just the one potentially time-consuming task in her regular task section. Every other task for the week is optional: each of them can be moved or abandoned altogether if there is too little time by the end of the week.

Week nine

Regular RESIDENTIAL STUDY SCHOOL
tutorial on graduate training programmes essay – make notes to prepare for it
Wish revision cards for module B
Extra website study chat room – Friday

During this week our student is intending to spend most of the week focusing on the outside world, rather than learning alone. The residential study school begins the week, and she intends to make notes to prepare for her tutorial (to be held during the study school) whilst she is travelling by train to the school. She also hopes to produce some revision cards for an earlier module on the train journey home on Sunday night. Beyond this, she is determined to do nothing more than spend some time with her family, and spend her spare moments not producing more work, but just thinking through the issues that have been raised at the study school and making some notes to back up her notes from the day. She can then log onto the course website chat room on Friday night, ready to discuss the study school and follow up contacts and research leads.

Week ten

Regular re-enrol on counselling skills course
begin work-based study
work out new personalised timetable
Wish time out at home
update reading and research notebooks
Extra

In an ideal situation, this week will be a pleasure, as our student spends time at work on her work-based study, and confines her home time studying to 'spring cleaning' her studying, perhaps by re-enrolling on a course, working out her next personalised timetable or updating her reading and research notebooks. This will give her the breathing space she needs before embarking on her next personalised timetable.

In reality, of course, this week might be quite different, if she has been forced to reschedule many of her tasks and they have all ended up in this last week. If this happens to you, you might consider extending your personalised timetable by a week at this stage, just listing all the 'catch-up' tasks that you must either try to complete or abandon during that week. It is because tasks can accumulate at the end of a personalised timetable like this that producing a new timetable every eight to ten weeks is a good idea: it allows you to assess whether you are being too ambitious and to tailor your next personalised timetable to suit your circumstances.

If you need to make changes because your personalised timetable is not working well, there are several guidelines to follow:

- consider designating every fourth week as a catch-up week, in which you will work however hard you have to in order to tackle all the unfinished tasks.
- you might include a 'reading week' in your personalised timetable, during which you will focus exclusively on catching up with your reading lists, leaving you more time during other weeks to produce assignments and work through assessment tests.
- if you find it difficult to work in all directions at once, you might produce a skeleton timetable that only includes essential tasks, such as assignments, and then give over certain weeks exclusively to the completion of each of these tasks. You can then diversify your workload by adding other tasks to your personalised timetable in other weeks when you are under less pressure.
- assess whether you are using your personalised timetable as a dumping ground for those tasks you never really intend to complete. It can be a relief to tick tasks off your mental list of 'things to do' by placing them on your personalised timetable, but you then risk these tasks accumulating at the end of the personalised timetable, where they will be no more palatable. Instead of doing this, each time you come to review your personalised timetable check whether there are any tasks that could sensibly be taken out, either because they have now become irrelevant or you know they are not vital and you will never actually manage to complete them.

Your relationship with your tutor, mentor and supervisor

Developing productive relationships with your tutor, mentor and supervisor will be crucial to the successful management of your distance and open learning course, yet some students find this difficult. This is not necessarily because they find talking to their tutors difficult, but because they are confused over the boundaries of the different working relationships they are trying to develop, and unclear about what is on offer. This is understandable, as course literature is often vague about this aspect of distance and open learning courses and different terms are used for similar roles on different courses. The terms given to describe those who will support you in your course can be used interchangeably, but to reduce the confusion, the most commonly used terms are defined here in the way in which they are most usually used:

- *Lecturer*: this is a term applied to anyone teaching on your course, whether or not you actually receive lectures as part of your course. In many distance and open learning courses the term is no longer used. Your contact with lecturers might be limited to working through their tutor packs or meeting them during residential schools or study sessions and workshops, with some email backup if you are working on an assignment that relates to their field of expertise.
- *Tutor*: it would not be unusual for all those delivering your course to be called tutors, although the term also applies to specific staff whose role it is to support you in a wider sense throughout your course. These tutors might be called 'personal', 'pastoral' or 'lead' tutors and they will be on hand to guide you through the course and support you in a multitude of ways as you progress through the learning process. It is with this type of tutor that this section is primarily concerned.
- *Mentor*: your mentor might not be directly involved in the delivery of your course, but might be a professional in your field whose role is to support your learning as part of your professional development. Your mentor might be your line manager or the training manager within your workplace, or a professional drafted in from a professional body in order to help you to link your learning and your professional development.
- *Supervisor*: you might not need the support of a supervisor, whose role is usually to guide students through research, such as in the preparation of a dissertation or the working out of a long-term research assignment.

You might not expect to have problems developing a relationship with any of these course contacts, but there are three principal reasons why it is a good idea to give the situation some thought in the early stages of your course. Firstly, you will want to ensure that you are getting the best possible support by asking the most appropriate person for help in a variety of situations. Secondly, if you hit a moment of crisis and need help in a hurry, you will not want to waste time trying to locate that help. Lastly, if you are unsure about the sort of help that you can expect from different contacts, you can lose confidence in the process, and find yourself reluctant to ask for help in case you are asking the wrong person, or asking someone to work outside their normal remit. Before examining each of these relationships in some detail, it is worth considering three factors that will affect all of them: experience, availability and personality.

Experience

Although it is logical to assume that the more experience your contacts have, both as academics and distance and open learning experts, the more help they can offer you, this is not always the case. An experienced contact will be familiar with the system and so will be in a good position to support you; an established academic or professional with a reputation will also be able to help you with your academic networking and, perhaps, with your future career. However, such a contact might be in great demand, with many distance and open learners to work with at any one time, and this might leave you feeling as if you are permanently in a queuing system taking up time for which others are competing. A less experienced contact may not be so familiar with all aspects of your field, but you might benefit from an energetic, fresh approach to the tutor/tutee relationship and an enthusiastic commitment to getting it right. When considering your contact's expertise, try to think not just of the overall subject area of your course, but also your particular area of experience and interest in terms of long-term research. You might decide to choose an academic contact who is strong on aspects of the course with which you are less familiar, knowing that you can rely on others (such as your professional mentor) for more specialist help with your research. You might find aspects of distance and open learning particularly daunting, and so will want your contact to be experienced in these fields rather than necessarily being an expert principally in your specialist subject area. All these factors need to be taken into account as you work with your contact.

Availability

Within a distance and open learning course you do not have the advantage of being able to have face-to-face sessions with your contact at a moment's notice. On the other hand, you will be able to communicate with your contact regularly in ways that are not always open to full-time students on a campus-based course, so this need not be a difficulty. The availability of support, whether you have chosen your contact or not, is going to be critical to your working patterns, so you need to analyse how you work best and then find out if support is available to help you in the most productive way possible. Some contacts are happy to talk on the telephone with their students out of office hours, some restrict this support to daytime hours only. Some prefer to offer email support, whilst others regularly visit the online study site chat room and message board area to provide online support. There are contacts who deliberately make themselves as available as possible during study schools, whilst others arrange face-to-face seminars and workshop sessions outside the normal structure of the course. None of these approaches is necessarily any better than the others, but one might suit your needs best. The issue of availability must be tackled as early as possible, before you find yourself in situation where you need to get hold of your contact in a rush. If your course literature is not clear about this, email your contact in the first few weeks of your course to ask how best he or she likes to communicate. You will not be considered a nuisance for asking such a practical question, and the answer you get will give you all the information that you need to plan your support structure.

Personality

This is a difficult one. Your contact may not become a friend; indeed, this might not be a good idea if you want to make the most of the relationship. You might not discuss your personal lives at all (unless these are relevant to your progress) and this is perfectly normal and no hindrance to a productive working relationship. However, if you find your contact a difficult person to get along with, or you find that the methods that are being used to supervise you are counterproductive, this will hinder your relationship. This is nobody's fault, but you do need to consider the basics of how you learn best before you decide that one contact is better for you than another. Do you find it easy to talk through research problems? Are you confident enough to voice your ideas at a study school or in a workshop setting? Do you find explanations offered to you by email easy to understand, or are you better working face to face or on the telephone? Are you easily intimidated by experts in your field? If you can work through this series of questions, you will be able to analyse the problem and decide whether you are really unsuited to your contact, or whether (as is more likely to be the case) you are finding the means of support on your distance and open learning course difficult. If your contact only ever communicates with students by email and is never available on the end of the telephone, or alternatively offers support in workshops and never responds to email, you might have to consider asking for a change in contact, but this will only be the best course of action if you have explored all avenues with your contact and tutor before making this move.

This checklist for a contact overlooks the most important characteristic of any potential contact: enthusiasm. If your contact is happy to work with you, keen and ready to support your efforts and prepared to spend time thinking about your needs, finding information for you and pointing you in the right direction, then you are in the fortunate position of knowing that you will have a staunch ally in the management of your course. Whether or not you are able to choose your contacts, it is important to take an active part in these relationships from the outset. To begin with, you need to ask yourself some questions: what are your expectations? What do you need from your contact? What are you able to offer to the learning process? How might you ensure that the relationship runs smoothly? If you can set your own agenda and work with your contact from the outset with a clear idea of what you will need and what you think you can reasonably expect, you will save yourself valuable time and effort in the future and minimise the possibility of confusion. You will not rely equally on all these relationships at all points in your course. As your work progresses, your needs will change, and the guidelines below will help you to continue to benefit as fully as possible from each relationship.

Your lecturers

Whether or not the staff providing study material for your course are called lecturers or regular tutors, several factors will affect your management of these relationships: availablitiy, asumptions, preparation, support and tutorials.

Availability

This will be limited, as your relationship will often be 'virtual', that is, the result of working through a tutor pack or receiving online support for assignments and research projects. This need not be a negative factor in the relationship; it simply means that you have to remain focused on the support you need and be clear about communicating your needs to your lecturers and tutors.

Assumptions

Try to avoid the assumption that every lecturer or regular tutor on your course will be available as part of your course structure. It may be that professionals who are not the principal course providers have been brought in to produce some of the course material, so your contact with them may be limited by their peripheral involvement in the course. If this is the case, the majority of your queries will be rerouted through your course providers, but you can be sure that if you have a query there will be someone there to help you, even if the support does not come directly from the lecturer or tutor who produced the initial material.

Preparation

If you are in a position to meet your lecturers or regular tutors, perhaps at a workshop session or study school, it is essential that you prepare well. Distance and open learning courses can sometimes seem a little disjointed, and students can arrive at day schools having carried out very little preparation, because they were so busy working through one assignment that they overlooked the fact that the day school was intended to provide support for a different assignment. This can lead to confusion as students ask questions that the lecturer on the day might be ill-equipped to answer. In some cases students save all their queries on the course in its entirety for these occasions, usually because they are uncertain about where to go for help on a day-to-day basis. This can result in students gaining only a fraction of the help that is on offer on the day, as they are preoccupied with different learning outcomes from those intended for the day. The safest way to approach this is to read the details of any contact time carefully and assume that you will only be offered support in the area that has been designated for the day. In this way you can guarantee the highest level of support and avoid wasting your energy and time on queries that cannot be dealt with fully on that occasion.

Support

Distance and open learning course providers are usually passionate about their courses and enthusiastic about their students, which can lead to lecturers with only a minimal input into a course trying to answer every question that is put to them, even if they are not expert in that particular field, or completely confident about the aspect of the course structure that is being queried. It is for this reason that you can employ the useful management tool of prefacing each query with the question 'are you the best person to ask about this point?' and the suggestion that you would be happy to ask someone else if this would be preferable. This will allow the lecturer or regular tutor to take stock of the situation and refer you to someone else if necessary and it will reassure you that the information you receive if the lecturer does answer the query is both up to date and comprehensive.

Tutorials

Although you may have limited contact with lecturers or regular tutors, you might occasionally have very focused time together if they have been involved in marking your work or monitoring one of your self-assessment exercises. During this time, you might meet to discuss the mark or assessment, or you might communicate through the course website, by email or telephone. Within this framework, you will need to prepare for the situation, by working through the assignment or self-assessment tests and noting any queries you have about the comments made or the marks you have been given. This is a time for highlighting problems with that specific assignment and identifying any challenges you face that might have a wider impact upon your progress. If you do identify more wide-ranging problems, you will again be asking whether this lecturer or general tutor is the right person to help you, or whether you might be better to note the problem, discuss it within the context of this assignment or self-assessment test and then move on to get help elsewhere in the long term.

Your tutors

Tutors are the support staff with whom you might have the most contact: it is common for distance and open learners to be allocated a personal tutor (or pastoral tutor, individual tutor, lead tutor or academic tutor) for the duration of their course. As with lecturers and regular tutors, you will need to be clear about the ways in which your course provider expects this relationship to work. The key point is to consider the logistics of your contact with your tutor. This might range from electronic support in the form of email and study chat rooms, to workshops and seminar sessions during which a group of you will work together with your tutor, to one-to-one sessions either in person or on the telephone to discuss a specific piece of work or consider your progress on the course as a whole. There are several areas where your designated tutor will be best placed to support you: assignments, networking, your course profile and emotions.

Assignments

Your tutor can help you to develop the shape of an assignment and guide your research. A tutor is also in a good position to help you with practical queries on assignments, such as word count and the layout of your bibliography, as well as helping you to arrange extensions of the deadlines for assignments if you run into difficulties. You will be expecting this support, but do not be surprised if you are asked to produce some written work in preparation for any contact time you have together. Tutors on distance and open learning courses are aware that they have relatively little face-to-face time with students compared to the work that you are putting into your course and they will want to make the most of the time you do have together. For this reason, you might be asked to produce a written record of your activities, or a draft plan of your next assignment, before you meet.

If you are busy trying to fit your studying into an already hectic life, this level of preparation can seem like a waste of time, particularly if your next assignment is not due to be completed for several weeks, but it will always be to your benefit. The art of successfully managing a course is largely the result of keeping your ideas flowing and continually making connections between different areas of your course. By producing an assignment plan or recording your studying activities and plans in advance of your meeting, you are forcing yourself to practise articulating your ideas in writing and you will be creating a valuable record of how your ideas are developing. Trying out ideas in this way is always more satisfactory than just jotting them down in the margins of your notes, and it will ensure that your tutor is fully aware of your intentions and so can guide you effectively through the next stage of your studying. There is a further benefit to this process: when you come to write up your assignment, you will have a record not only of your plan but also notes on how your tutor reacted to the plan and this will help to guide you as to the overall shape of your assignment.

You might also want to send your tutor a copy of your personalised timetable before you get together, so that you are both clear about the ways in which you are dividing your time and planning your studying. This will obviously have a positive impact on your tutor, who will be able to appreciate how organised you are, but will also benefit you because your tutor will have had the time to consider your plan and so can offer constructive suggestions as to how you might streamline your studying or alter your plan to include activities that will directly benefit you in your skills development planning.

Networking

We all tend to network instinctively within our professional lives, but distance and open learners can overlook the value of this within their studying. Even if you are not intending to pursue your studying beyond your current course, networking through your tutor is useful in many ways. Your tutor might, for example, know of a student who is working on a tangential field of study to yours and who could share research sources with you, or a student who faces similar challenges to your own and with whom you can arrange some mutual support.

Sometimes your networking will be less specific. Perhaps you would like to meet regularly with other distance and open learners in your area, share lifts to relevant conferences or perhaps you have heard of a discussion group that is being set up but the details of which are hazy. Your tutor is there to help with these aspects of networking, as well as ensuring that you do not become isolated in your studying.

Your course profile

The great appeal of distance and open learning courses is that they allow you so much flexibility. At regular points throughout each course students are in a position to make choices about the options they want to take and decide how their research might develop. However, it is easy to work through a course without ever fully assessing just how flexible it is and how much choice you really have. At best, this can lead to you completing a course without having made it as personally relevant to your interests or professional development as you might have done. At worst, you can find yourself working through a course module which has a limited appeal for you. If you include in your personalised timetable a plan to assess your course regularly, making choices about how it might develop as you decide between different modules, then you will be in a good position to avoid these difficulties. If you then also make a note to talk to your tutor on a regular basis about the options open to you, you will know that you have done everything possible to make your course as flexible, relevant and interesting as possible.

The situation can be similar if you are undertaking a major piece of research as part of your course. The plan for your research will alter over time, with perhaps a growing emphasis on one area, or the addition of a new section as additional material comes to light. This is a normal part of the creative process and should cause you no great concern. However, there might come a time when you begin to feel that a radical new direction is needed, your base hypothesis is flawed or inadequate and you will not being doing justice to your work until you make a change in direction, perhaps by altering the thrust of your plan entirely. This will not be an overnight decision. Instead, you will probably spend time with a general feeling of unease as you find that each area on which you are working seems to support your new ideas more than your existing plan. Try not to allow this stage to extend beyond a couple of weeks. When, eventually, you decide to take the plunge and make a new plan, avoid the temptation to develop it fully and work all your material into it before sharing it with your tutor. It is far better to arrange a meeting or set up an email discussion to explore this new direction when you have no more than a draft revised plan in place. In this way your tutor can guide you through the changes you want to make and discuss with you how your material will fit into the new plan.

There are two other reasons for revealing to your tutor a change of direction relatively early in the process. You might be surprised at just how much time a dedicated tutor will spend thinking about your work: each article that he or she reads, or seminar or conference that he or she attends, could throw up suggestions ready for your next meeting or email discussion. It is therefore frustrating for your tutor to find that you changed your mind about the overall direction of your research but have not mentioned it. Secondly, a change of direction might require a level of extended supervision, either by email or face to face, whilst you work through the plan together, or the bringing in of an additional tutor or professional advisor from another area, and these things take time to arrange, time which you will not want to waste.

Emotional support

Ideally you will breeze through your distance and open learning course, with never a doubt about your direction and a lasting certainty about both your abilities and the shape that your course is taking. In practice, your learning experience is likely to be a mixture of two extremes. There will be times when you feel on top of the course (and so on top of the world) and everything is falling into place with seemingly very little effort. At other points on your journey you will inevitably feel less sure of yourself and your studying, unclear of your overall aims and uncertain as to where to go next. At both these points your tutor should be an asset to you. When things are going well, you will have the time and energy to discuss your future, new avenues of research or your skills development strategy. When things are going badly, your contact will offer you practical and academic guidance and also a level of emotional support.

The key to managing this potentially awkward aspect of the relationship is to get into the habit of communicating regularly and speak up when you feel vulnerable. You do not have the luxury of being able to see your tutor regularly on a casual basis face to face, but you can overcome this. Your tutor will be used to supporting students via email or the telephone and you will become used to this too, particularly if you already have a relationship in place because you have kept in contact by reporting on your progress when things were going well. If distance and open learning tutors can feel that they know their students well before things go wrong, they are in a far better position to be of real help to them when things are going less well.

You might also believe, mistakenly, that your relationship with your tutor is a constant test of your capabilities, and any problems you share with your tutor will be seen as evidence of weakness or lack of ability on your part. This is simply not true. The more you strive to appear to be on top of things, even when you feel that things are falling apart, the less inclined your tutor will be to offer what might seem to be unnecessary emotional encouragement. In fact, we all need praise and reassurance, however organised we are, so make this clear to your tutor, who may feel diffident about this area. If you ask for encouragement ('Do you really think that this approach worked?' 'I found this assignment so much harder to do than I had expected.' 'Although I look organised, I have slaved for hours over just this one essay.'), then your tutor will know that you welcome emotional support. Your tutor is not a mind-reader, and may genuinely think that you are having no problems, you would shun too much encouragement or you are unapproachable because you appear to be so organised. If none of these statements is true of you, make sure that you tutor knows, or you might be left feeling needlessly isolated.

Your mentor

A mentor might not be directly involved in the delivery of your study material and so might, to some extent, be outside the structure of your course, but this is not to suggest that he or she is any less valuable in supporting your efforts than your course providers. Your mentor is likely to be a professional colleague or an expert assigned to you because of his or her experience in your field of interest. There are several areas where your mentor might be crucial to the successful management of your course: course relevance, availability, practical support, asumptions and career development.

The relevance of your course

The ways in which a course is relevant to their professional life, now and in the future, are not always immediately obvious to distance and open learners, particularly if they are studying a subject with which they are only newly familiar. A mentor will be able to show you how the academic work you are undertaking can have an impact on your professional outlook. Having a mentor in place is such an excellent way to advance your interests that it would be worthwhile seeking out a mentor even if your course provider does not include mentors as part of your course package.

Availability

Whilst your contact time with your tutor might be limited, working with a mentor can ensure that you have regular and relatively casual support in place when you need it. Minor subject queries can be addressed to your mentor, whereas you might hesitate to spend precious time with your tutor on these issues. If you are working alongside your mentor in a professional capacity, much of your conversation will soon be taken up with your course and its impact on your working life, and this will help you to see the interconnectivity of your studying and working life. You will not want your mentor to take over the role of your tutor, but the emotional support that you can gain from a mentor can make a positive difference to the way you feel about your course.

Practical support

It is sometimes difficult to know where to go for help with practical studying difficulties, such as how to expand your reading list in an area, how to cover your travelling costs if you want to attend a conference or how to put a plan for a research-based project into practice. Although your course provider will help wherever possible, your mentor might be well placed to give you practical help of this sort.

Assumptions

It can be easy to confuse the role of your various course contacts. Your mentor will be invaluable in many ways, but may not be familiar with every aspect of your course and its requirements. You are working through a course of study that might ask you to undertake tasks in a way that differs from the norm within your profession, and you must be on your guard against ignoring the requirements of your course in favour of the ways of working adopted by your mentor. For example, when you are set an assignment, you may be asked to produce a report in a specific format, one that is internationally recognised in your field. This may not be the format you have used within your working life, and it is tempting simply to produce the report as you would usually do, on the assumption that this must be acceptable. This will not be the case, and you may fail the assignment as a result, so in cases like this you need to ensure that you follow the guidelines laid down by your course provider rather than assuming that your mentor's way is preferable.

Career development

Your tutors and lecturers may be guiding you towards future courses and suggesting ways in which each course might further your career, but your mentor is also in a good position to support you in this area. You will have talked openly about your experience on the course (perhaps more candidly than you have felt able to talk to your tutors) and so your mentor will know which ways of working suit you best and which areas are of interest to you for the future. Do not overlook the networking potential of this relationship: your mentor will not only be helping you as your course progresses, but will also have one eye on your future career, and it makes sense to reap the career benefits of this relationship.

Your supervisor

A supervisor will usually be assigned to you only if you are undertaking a research-based project, such as a major research assignment or a dissertation. Your supervisor might be your mentor or your personal tutor, but is just as likely to be another contact within your course structure. Your work with your supervisor will be limited to working together on your assignment; you will still turn to your tutors for overall guidance on your course and help with other assignments. Your relationship with your supervisor is going to be fundamental to your success within your research-based project and it will work best if you have identified the areas in which you can expect to receive help: supervisions, research skills, ethics and ideas.

Supervisions

These are one-to-one sessions (very occasionally, they may include several students), conducted either face to face or via email, during which your supervisor will talk through the specific challenges you are facing. This might include talking about the overall shape of your dissertation or other research assignment, or the direction in which you are moving within one particular area of your research. They are your chance to get the highest possible level of support for your work, so be prepared to ask questions and seek clarification about anything that remains unclear to you. Your early sessions might be quite general in nature, so they should not be viewed as a test of some sort: they are wholly for your benefit and should be seen as such.

The secret of successful supervisions is to prepare yourself for them in advance by reviewing your plan, updating your reading and research notebooks and outlining the questions you need to ask. In this way you are able to take some control of the supervision process and ensure that each session answers your specific questions: it is a time in which your supervisor should be fully focused on your needs, your ideas and the challenges you face; supervisions will come to underpin everything you do. As your time together might be limited, make sure that you back up each supervision with an email outlining your understanding of what has been suggested and agreed. This will give your supervisor the chance to think through the research again, correct any misunderstandings and make further suggestions. It will also provide a starting point for future discussions.

Research skills

Nobody is going to assume that you are already an expert on producing a dissertation or working through a major research assignment: you have yet to do this. Equally, you will not be expected to come up with the last word in your area: good research tends to raise as many questions as it answers. However, you already have a recognised skills base, to which you are adding as your learning progresses, and your course will have been designed to ensure that you become proficient in articulating your ideas in a variety of formats. What you may feel less confident about is the process of undertaking lengthy research and presenting it coherently. Where do you go for material? How can you remain focused? What should you discard? How can you tell if a theory has been discredited and are there credible alternatives to it? How will you be able to produce a workable plan? How can you ensure that a work-based project is relevant and successful? In addition to these general questions, you might have your own specific areas of concern: how can you improve your writing skills? How do you prepare to give a research presentation? How can you make the most of the internet and CD-ROM resources? Make a note of these issues as they arise and bring them up with your supervisor.

Embarrassment is the greatest single hindrance to a productive relationship with your supervisor. You might feel shy about revealing that you have a problem with grammar or spelling, but your supervisor can easily point you in the direction of study skills workshops that will help with your problem. You are not going to be familiar with the work of every leading expert in your field, indeed you may not have heard of several of them, but your supervisor will expect this and be happy to expand your reading plan with you. You might assume that you should know exactly where to go next in your research, but why should you? You are not the expert, but your supervisor is, and it is this expertise that you must rely upon.

Ethics

It is not always easy to grasp the complete range of ethical considerations that you will need to take into account as your work progresses, particularly if you have not worked within an educational discipline for some time, but your supervisor will be acutely aware of this issue and will be able to offer you valuable advice. Although, in some areas, a clearly defined code of ethics will apply (for example if you are using human tissue within scientific experimentation or using data drawn from individuals within social science research), in other areas of activity there might be less clarity. The best way to approach this is to assume that, even if you are aware of an ethical or professional code of practice in your area, it is still advisable to discuss this issue with your supervisor as your work develops, particularly as you might need ethical approval from your course provider or professional body to carry out certain elements of your research. If you are in any way uncertain about the ethical implications of your work, do not rely solely upon written guidelines, but use them in conjunction with the advice and experience that your supervisor can offer you.

Ideas

Your supervisor may or may not be good at coming up with ideas. Some supervisors seem to have endless reserves of inspiration, whilst others will simply reflect upon the ideas that you generate. Supervisors with plenty of ideas can help to maintain your interest in, and commitment to, your research. On the downside, inspirational supervisors might lack the attention to detail and considered reflection of your work that you need. A positive benefit of a reflective supervisor might that you are given plenty of support about how to turn your ideas into workable hypotheses. If you know that you are the sort of person who finds it difficult to get out of a mindset that is going nowhere and you will need to be fed lots of ideas as you go along, but your supervisor is not an 'ideas person', take control of the situation. If you can produce a few ideas yourself, however sketchy or tangential to your research, this will encourage your supervisor to join with you in thinking up more. Even if your supervisor is not naturally very creative you will find that experience tells, and ideas or theories that are familiar to your supervisor will be new and exciting to you.

Never be put off by the fact that your contact with your supervisor might be restricted to email or telephone calls, with only rare face-to-face sessions. This need not hinder you at all, as long as you work at developing a close working relationship. It is only natural that you will feel reluctant about pestering your supervisor, and so might hesitate to email revised plans or lists of new ideas every few days, but it is wise to make contact on a weekly basis, even if only to let your supervisor know that things are going according to plan. In this way you will be overcoming the potential problems of supervision from a distance even before they arise. You can 'talk' to your tutor at any time via email, so the distance is not real, it just becomes real in your mind if you allow it to.

Having read through this section of the chapter, you might be struck by the fact that the practical queries you may be encountering on your course have only been touched upon rather than discussed in detail. This is because one vital source of support has not been discussed, the one relationship that you must manage with more finesse than any other: your relationship with the administrative support staff on your distance and open learning course. They are the backbone of any course. They know precisely where to find the elusive missing reading list, they can tell you exactly when each assignment is due in and they are familiar with the routine of each tutor on the course; they have even been known to fix the course website when the technical support staff take too long to arrive. Never underestimate the help they can give you, both in terms of the guidance they can offer over practical queries on the course, and in the time they can save you. If you have a query regarding your course and you have been waiting some time for an answer from your tutors or supervisor, give them a ring and simply ask. They will probably know the answer and if they are not sure, they will make sure that you get a response, fast.

With so many people to help you, it can be confusing trying to decide who to approach in the first instance with a query or problem. Your personal tutor will be your final destination if you cannot resolve the issue, but it might save you time to approach other support staff with some queries; it will also leave your time with your tutor free for more productive discussions. The table below lists ten of the most common problems for distance and open learning students and makes suggestions as to who it might be best to approach initially for help.

Problem	**Who to approach**
You are not sure which course packs relate to which modules	*Course secretary*, who will have a schedule of study packs and modules
Your computer is working fine, but you cannot access a course website	*IT services* (usually found in the library or resource centre, or online if you can access any of the course sites)
You have missed a broadcast that relates to your course	*Course secretary*, who will usually hold copies of broadcasts
You will not be able to meet a deadline	*Module tutor* who is to mark the assignment; it is usually relatively easy to extend a deadline
You might have to miss a residential study school or day school	*Course secretary* in the first instance, to discover if there is another school that you could attend instead

(*continued*)

Your project seems to be veering away from your initial plan	*Personal or module tutor*, as early as possible, with a revised plan to show clearly where you are going
You have failed in a self-assessment test	*Your study partner or study group online*, to check whether this is a general problem: then retake the test
You need to take time away from your course	*Personal tutor or supervisor*, with a clear idea of how long you will need to be away from the course, and why
Your reading lists are confusing you	*Course secretary*, to discover who compiled the lists so you can contact that tutor directly for more guidance
Your work-based project is going wrong	*Mentor*, who will have a breadth of experince in your area and will bring in your tutor if necessary

Every distance and open learning course has its own unique ways of working with students, guiding them through the learning process and helping them to produce the most effective and successful work. Some of the suggestions offered in this section will be more relevant to you than others, some of the terms will differ from one course to another, support structures will vary, but the underlying principle of this guidance remains the same: you need to master the structural elements of your course and the time you have available and you must take a positive approach to your relationship with your course contacts. If you are proactive in your attitude, demonstrating that you are actively planning your learning process and working towards an agreed goal, you will ensure that your relationship with all your course contacts is as productive as possible. As a distance and open learner you are not a passive recipient of information: you are a partner in the learning process, and the key to managing your course lies with the successful management, on both sides, of these vital relationships.

Spot guide

The key points to remember from this chapter:

- preparation in advance of your course will make the early stages more manageable
- take control of your course materials before they overwhelm you
- monitor your work rate and vary your study tasks
- creating a personalised timetable will be essential to the management of your course: start working on it early and revise it regularly
- successful time management relies on structuring your time, working within your personalised timetable and remaining flexible in your approach
- taking a break from studying can be a constructive move as long as you plan ahead and return to studying in an organised way
- learn what you can expect from each of your course contacts and remember that these are two-way relationships which can be developed as your needs change

5 Supporting your Learning Experience

Troubleshooting guide

Use this chapter for help if:

- you are getting behind with your reading
- you find reading lists confusing or overwhelming
- you make notes in a haphazard way or find them difficult to use
- you suspect that you are missing connections within your subject area
- you are confused about your research tasks or assignment preparation
- you feel that your workload is out of control
- your response to every crisis is just to work harder
- you are feeling demoralised and need to develop new studying strategies
- you want to succeed in workshop sessions, discussion groups, research teams and group presentations
- you like the idea of working with a study partner

Once you have put in place the structures to manage your studying, you can focus upon the day-to-day practicalities of mastering the learning process. These are similar for all students, and include learning to read effectively, make notes on a variety of sources and make connections between aspects of your course. Underpinning all this work will be the support systems that you put in place as your course progresses. These aspects of working as a distance and open learner will be essential to your success.

Reading effectively

Reading effectively is a vital skill that you will need to develop, particularly as distance and open learning courses rely heavily upon their students being able to take in information in this way. You will be given a series of reading lists and you will also develop your own lists as your course develops, based upon the tutorial material that you have been sent, the information that you glean from the internet and sources that are discussed during study schools and workshop sessions. It is tempting to create huge reading lists for yourself that you will never have the time to master, and this is demotivating. Take the example of one book or journal that you find useful. You feel that the author had really grasped this aspect of your subject and so you take copious notes and are inspired to read more. You turn to the bibliography or 'suggested reading' pages of the publication, only to find that there are perhaps 20–30 books and articles listed (sometimes many more) and you have the task of wading through this list, trying to make sensible decisions about which books to read and which to discard. What is certain is that you cannot read them all, so you have to make a choice. You will base this choice upon the relevance of the books and articles on offer and the date of publication. You may not discard a book simply because it was published years ago, but you will be more concerned to ensure that its contents are still relevant today. If you are tempted to work through too many books, you might usefully discipline yourself to photocopy the chapters in some books that are useful to you as you find them, rather than simply placing each book on your reading list and then losing track of how much of each book you will have to read.

Faced with your personalised reading list, you will see straightaway that much of your studying life will be made up of reading; not just reading, but also selecting, analysing, assimilating material and using it judiciously. Simply working your way methodically through your reading list, taking each book in its entirety and giving equal weight to each source, is not the best way forward. You will already know about your preferred style of reading (slow and steady, fast and furious, patchy but productive), but life as a distance and open learner will demand that you learn to skim read effectively, work steadily through some texts and read at speed whilst taking notes when the pressure is on.

There are books available to help you to expand your range of reading skills, but the key to managing your reading is to recognise that, at any one time, you are likely to have up to five different sorts of reading material to hand, each sort making different demands upon your skills:

1. You might have *recommended, principal texts* with which you will become familiar over the course of your study, texts that are widely considered to be the seminal works of reference in your field. These texts might not be books at all, but instead the tutor packs that you are sent, which you will treat in the same way as principal texts. Distance and open learning course providers tend to try to keep these to a minimum, aware that their students are already investing heavily in their course and unwilling to burden them with the cost of too many textbooks. If it is not made clear to you which books you should put in this category and go out and buy, it is always worth checking with your tutor or with other students via the course website before you buy them. The secret with these texts is not to let them overwhelm you or feel that they represent the last word in an area of research. You will begin to read them in the first few weeks of your course, and this should, of course, be done with some care, but you need not force yourself to understand every paragraph, or pressurise yourself to grasp every concept in its entirety. You will be revisiting these texts frequently, and their contents will be supported by tutorial material, the course website and perhaps television and radio broadcasts, so you will be reading them knowing that you will assimilate their contents in stages as your understanding increases.
2. You will have *essential backup reading* to do. Some of these texts will be on your reading lists, but you will probably also include your own texts if, for example, you are relying on a basic, general text to support your growing understanding of a new area of study. As I have mentioned before, there is no need to be hesitant about asking for such a text: your course providers will not expect you to have extensive experience in every field, and will be able to recommend good, basic guides in each aspect of your course. Your relationship with these texts might be short-lived, particularly if you are using a text just to support one area of your course; you may decide to buy some of them, but you will want to work with them for a time before deciding whether to invest in them as permanent resources. The reading skills involved in using them will be different from those demanded by the principal, set texts. You will be approaching them with your particular research or assignment requirements in mind, and with an awareness of what is contained within your principal texts. You are much more likely, therefore, as you make notes on these books, to be arguing with some of the premises contained within them and comparing theories. This reading is much more active in many ways. You are not expected to soak up the book in its entirety, but rather you are asked to use it as an aid to sharpen your argument and deepen your understanding.

3. You will be using some texts as a very *immediate aid* in producing a specific piece of work. These texts are often (and sometimes most usefully) collections of essays or specialist journals. Reading essay collections is the quickest way to assess whether you have covered all the current aspects of a field of study: they are also a great way to familiarise yourself with the arguments that range around a subject, without you needing to examine every single facet of it yourself in depth. You are unlikely to read these books or journals from cover to cover and you will be skim reading many of them; you might simply browse through the index in order to find the one or two references within the text that may be of use to you. These are also the texts from which you are most likely to be photocopying sections or even single pages. It is far easier to attach a photocopied section to your own notes than to make extensive notes of your own, but there are two points to remember whilst you do this. Firstly, make sure that you make an exact and extensive note of the title, author and publication details of the text on your photocopy. Remember that you are going to be creating your own bibliographies for your assignments, and there is nothing more frustrating than having to waste valuable time in the library trying to hunt out a book to which you wish to refer, but the details of which you forgot to take at the time. It can also be disastrous, if you have photocopied a section of a text that is now out on loan for three months.

   You also need to make sure that you take ownership of the information contained within the photocopied section or chapter. It is a lovely feeling to have spent the morning in the library, photocopying all sorts of useful information, and then to put all the photocopies neatly into plastics wallets in your files. Sadly, you may then ignore them for weeks or even months and then realise that you have no idea, when you come to look at them, why you ever thought that they were relevant, particularly if your course has taken a new turn since you first made the photocopies. You can also find that, because you have not highlighted the relevant sentences, you have to struggle through vast tracts of material before finding the one reference that you need. So, you must decide in advance to divide your time equally between identifying and finding the texts, photocopying the relevant sections and then highlighting the sections or sentences that you will need for future reference. Then you can put them in plastic wallets in your files, with their full references noted down, and feel truly virtuous.
4. You will have books that you have set aside for *leisure reading*. These might include the latest thrillers or romantic novels, but you will also have books that are dealing with issues on the periphery of your course,

texts that you will not expect to make extensive notes on, but that will be useful to you in terms of giving you background information. You will not make many notes on these texts: they are there to help you to immerse yourself in the atmosphere of the subject that you are studying. However, you will need to balance your leisure reading. If you know that you are the sort of reader who can never relax and so will leap up from your bed each night to make notes on the biography that is meant to be for leisure reading, or if you find that you will sleep badly if you read anything related to your course, then finish off with a good trashy novel each night, or allow yourself the time every now and then to read something in your leisure time that is entirely unrelated to your field.

5. The last set of books that might haunt you are those you feel you *ought to read*, even though they are too dense for you to get to grips with, or, as can happen, almost unreadable. It is easy to fall into the trap of thinking that, because you are studying, you really ought to be able to master every book that bears any relation to your subject area, yet this is simply not the case. Some authors write badly, whatever the subject, and the fact that you cannot master their work is thus their fault, not yours. Even with books written in an accessible style, you might be unable to master every concept or understand every viewpoint. Of course, you will want to understand all the major theories in your field, and make use of the concepts, ideas and viewpoints that are presented to you, but you are not a failure if a few stones are left unturned: talk to other students and your tutor to find out if this book is really essential to your success.

   The books that you simply cannot master tend to gravitate towards the bottom of your reading pile, and the management technique to employ here is to make yourself have a good clear out of your book pile at the end of each month. If you come across a book that has been sitting, unread, on the pile, be honest with yourself. Are you ever going to read it? Is it essential to the development of your learning? Is it enhancing your studying experience? If the answer to all these questions is no (and it probably will be), be ruthless with yourself and return the book firmly to the library. It will be available later if you suddenly need it, but at least it will not be in your sight all the time.

Once you have grasped that the huge pile of books loitering meaningfully in the corner of a room can in fact be divided into these five categories, you will feel far more in control. You know that some of the books will be read in their entirety over the course of a few weeks or months, but you also have the consolation of knowing that most of them will be read only partially, and in a very different style from the way in which you will approach your principal texts. Books viewed in this way become tools to be used in a variety of ways, not all of which are too time-consuming. You will be able to use your differing reading skills, plan your reading schedule according to your mood, work commitments and energy levels, and get on constructively with your studying. To help you to remain in control of your reading, the checklist below will remind you how to approach the texts on your course.

1. Recommended, principal texts:
- buy these and keep them with you throughout your course
- work through them slowly: there is plenty of time
- these will form the basis of your theoretical development within your subject

2. Essential backup reading:
- buy these only if you expect to use them extensively throughout your course
- analyse their value to you, be prepared to discard some sections that are of limited value on your course
- return to them as you plan assignments
- check the bibliographies for clues as to what else to read

3. 'Immediate aid' texts:
- you will not be reading these in their entirety
- become adept at scanning contents pages in the library before your take these books out
- photocopy the chapters you need and highlight the relevant sections if you are pushed for time
- scan the index and bibliography for guidance
- always keep a full record of the publication details

4. Leisure reading:
- decide early in your course whether this can be related in any way to your studying
- use your leisure reading as an escape from your other reading, and to keep your reading speed up

5. 'Ought to read' books:
- identify which books fall into this category for you
- be firm with them by checking the contents pages and index to see if you can extract anything from them

(continued)

- return them to the library once you have evaluated their worth
- ask your tutor for a further, related text if you need more help in the subject covered by the book
- never assume that it is your fault that a book was not conducive to your way of working

Making notes

The production of useful notes is an art in itself, one you might have developed in earlier study situations, but for a distance and open learner there is a danger in taking notes that is less pronounced for on-site students. They might be sitting in a lecture or seminar and so have a limited time in which to take notes: you are more likely to spend most of your time working through material on your own, and so could spend far too long or short a time in note taking. The danger lies in either producing notes that are almost as long as the original material, and then not being able to identify the salient points, or making notes that are so brief as to be of little value to you in the future. Some sense of the 'right' length of notes will come to you as your studying progresses, but as a distance and open learner you need to see your note taking as an active process, one that continues beyond the initial learning situation. You will be making notes from a variety of sources, and it will help you if you can keep the layout of your notes as uniform as possible, using a standard format to indicate books you must read, ideas you want to explore further and theories you want to consider.

The notes you take from any situation must show clearly the distinction between your ideas and those taken from elsewhere. This habit must be rigorously adopted and absolutely unbreakable throughout your course. Plagiarism is the gravest offence in the academic world, and most students would be indignant at the very suggestion that they would do such a thing, but you can find yourself mistakenly quoting a source without realising it if you are not careful to make your sources clear in every set of notes you make. This is particularly true of distance and open learning students, who are expected to use information from such a wide variety of sources. If you get into the habit of marking and naming your sources at every stage, you will protect yourself from any hint of plagiarism, which always reults in severe penalties.

You may have an initial set of notes that you have made on a tutor pack or from your internet study site, and these will be revisited periodically. It is a good idea to reduce some of these notes to key words on index cards and work through them periodically to reassess what they are offering you. This has two clear advantages. There will not be time when you are writing up a piece of work to wade through reams of undigested notes in the hope that you will be able to pick out rapidly the most useful points; by reworking your notes you will have to read through only a fraction of your initial work in order to locate those facts and ideas relevant to the task in hand. The second advantage is that reworking your notes will help you to focus. It will throw up new ideas, reaffirm theories you already hold and help you to avoid missing any learning opportunities.

Let us take as an example a set of notes made from a website dealing with the subject of publication in the seventeenth century. The website has been recommended to a student by the course providers because she intends to produce an assignment on female-authored publications in this period, but it is rather general in nature, so she will have to work to ensure that she extracts only relevant information from the website. She is an active note taker and has produced a relatively comprehensive set of notes which is reproduced here.

6th Dec 2003	Title: Publication in the seventeenth century
Dr Becker	Publications in C17 were usually of a religious nature.
website reference email address?	Many printers were involved: there was a need to make money, although some publications were printed at the expense of the author or his/her representatives. *Why? Commemoration? Family pride? Religious propaganda?*
	Popular ballads were produced in broadsheet format and sold cheaply to the masses. *How were women involved in this?*
	The advent of the printing press had made widespread publication possible.
INTRO	The tradition of manuscript circulation continued despite the development of print. *Am I going to include manuscripts? If not, mention it somewhere?*

(continued)

	It can be difficult to work out which authors wrote which books as they are often only identified by initials.
RESEARCH TASK	*Could be useful – go back and check on this . . .*
	Books were sometimes seen as monuments to the author, such as when a clergyman died and his sermons were published.
	My book on the subject mentions some issues of publication at this time.
READ THIS!!!	*What book?*
	Chapbooks were often said to be 'moral instruction manuals for the masses'. *Is this her quote? What are 'chapbooks'?*
	The Church was keen to take advantage of the possibilities of publication.
MY IDEA	*In a culture that mistrusted female speech, could women appear in print if they were supporting religious propaganda – was this a chance for them to be heard?*

As you can see, the website is only marginally useful to our student, but she has used it as a springboard to help her to focus on her next assignment. She has avoided the temptation to download the site in its entirety and will leave plenty of space between the points taken from the website (shown here in roman) so that she can add her own comments as her thoughts take shape (given here in italics). She has used the margin to organise the set of tasks that arise from this note taking session. By noting the date on which she studied the website and the exact reference for it, she can return to it easily, reference it in her bibliography and also decide whether other, more recent websites have superseded this one in terms of relevance and new research. She has made a note to check whether she can find out the email address of the website contributor, in case the website is updated or altered before she returns to it, or she needs to query a point that has been made. Even a general enquiry email address will usually produce a result. Some notes she can easily identify as being of use to her only as passing comments in her assignment, such as the 'intro' note, reminding her to mention whether or not she is using manuscript sources. Her research task will be entered into her research notebook (which will be discussed in detail later in this chapter) and her reading list will now include the book that was mentioned.

Perhaps the most important marginal note she has made is 'my idea'. It is so frustrating to see a clever idea in your notes and have no recollection, months after the event, whether it was yours or not. Plagiarism can leave you in the position of either having to go back and trace an idea (almost impossible, in many cases) or leaving it out of your work altogether, just in case you are plagiarising by mistake. By securing your own ideas in marginal notes in this way, you can use them with confidence and build upon them as your research progresses.

In addition to the marginal notes, our student has almost doubled her original extracts from the website with her own thoughts and instructions to herself. These instructions take the form of questions, reminding her to check on terms with which she is unfamiliar, suggesting new areas of source material she can explore and leading her to develop her existing ideas. Her initial notes would have been useful to her: these expanded notes will become the starting point for action.

Making connections

Being able to make meaningful and relevant connections between disparate pieces of studying is one of the most challenging aspects of a distance and open learning course, particularly as you may not be in a position to have these connections pointed out to you at every stage. You will have to make connections between what might often seem at first sight to be very unconnected pieces of material and this is where study groups, discussion sessions and your other study support groups could be valuable to you. The problem with trying to make connections as your work progresses is that, inevitably, if you fail to make a connection you have no idea that you have failed: after all, you have not made the connection because you did not notice it in the first place. There is a limit to the amount of connections you can make during your course, and there is no way to guarantee that you do not miss anything, but there are methods you can employ to ensure that you notice, and then use, most of the relevant connections available to you.

Keep research and reading notebooks

Your research and reading notebooks will become a steady source of inspiration to you, and will be discussed in detail in the next section. In the same way that your personalised timetable will help to keep you in control of your learning tasks, your reading and research notebooks will ensure that you do not lose the thread of your studying on a day-to-day basis.

Attend any event that might help you

You might not have time to attend every workshop session for your course, each professional development course or each conference that looks enticing. If you were to do this, your personalised timetable would soon become so full as to be of little real help to you. However, simply by looking around you and assessing what is being offered, by both your course provider and any professional body to which you belong, you will be in a far better position than most to make connections. This is particularly important if your course relies heavily on you working alone: becoming involved in a variety of learning opportunities will stop you feeling isolated, as well as helping you to make relevant connections.

Join discussion and study groups

The value of discussion and study groups has already been stressed, but you can do more than simply attend them. Even if you are not involved in running such a group, it is a good idea to suggest that those attending the group give short presentations, perhaps five minutes or so, on the progress of their studying. This might be a requirement of your course in any case, and these presentations will be useful to you. Although many of the presentations will be of no more than general interest, it will only take one or two passing comments to show you how the work of your fellow students could help to shape your own thoughts. These groups are so valuable to most students that it is worth considering starting up your own group if your course provider does not arrange them for you. This need not be an onerous task: even if you do not have the time to meet regularly with other students, or if you are geographically isolated, you will still be able to develop an email network fairly rapidly, as you are put in contact with other students; setting up an email discussion group will not be time-consuming and it will give you access to the connections made by other students in a relatively easy way.

Develop studying partnerships

Connections can sometimes be difficult to spot once you are embroiled in your subject, perhaps focused on writing an assignment or preparing for a seminar presentation. If you can find a studying partner, this will be one of the most valuable relationships within your distance and open learning course. By arranging to meet occasionally, either in person or on the internet, you can talk through the work you are doing. You need not both be studying on the same course: in fact, it can be more inspirational to get an outsider's opinion, so you might want to work in this way with a friend with whom you have studied in the past and whose work might now be taking a different direction from yours. It is a useful discipline to have to prepare something for these sessions, so that both of you get the chance to contribute and you do not run the risk of spending your time together simply discussing generalities. The questions your studying partner asks about your work ('Why is that so?', 'How do you know that this theory will work?', 'Is that the same point I was making in my last assignment?') will lead you to make connections you might not have seen by yourself.

Check contents pages, bibliographies and internet links

You will spend much of your studying time reading just part of each book that you discover or scouring the internet and journals for a single article. When you are doing this, try to pick up on the valuable connections that have already been made for you. By checking the contents page of a book or journal, you can see what other avenues have been explored in your subject area: if an author or journal editor has found connections, you might just as well use them. If you check the bibliography of a book, you might be surprised at how widely the author has read around the subject. Many of the texts included in a bibliography will be irrelevant to your needs, but if you spot a text that has no obvious connection with the book's contents, check it out, as it may be exploring an innovative new area within your field. If the website you are studying has a 'useful links' section, spend a *limited* amount of time browsing through these other sites, to see what the site authors feel is relevant and connected to their site. It is in these unlikely places that you can find really useful connections.

Make internet and catalogue connections

Although you will need to avoid spending too long browsing the internet in a haphazard way, it is worth occasionally spending 30 minutes or so browsing with a view to making connections. Type in your search term, either on the internet or a library cataloguing system, and see what comes up. Remember that you are not intending to read each site or look up each book, you are simply trying to see the connections that others have made within your subject area. By the end of the session you will have jotted down a series of random notes which will give you potential connections to bear in mind as you develop your ideas and add to your research notebook. Once you have worked through your ideas in more depth, you can return to the internet or catalogue to look in far more detail at the material on offer. This exercise also brings variety to your tasks, an advantage as you work through your basic studying tasks.

Mix disciplines

Making connections is all about keeping an open mind. We all become so used to working within a heavily defined sphere of reference that we can easily overlook the ways in which the work of other disciplines can enhance our own output. As a distance and open learner you will already have a positive and open view of your subject, and will be working to see how each aspect of your professional and studying life might fit together. Although this is not always an obvious path to tread, if you try to keep an open mind about the options available to you, it is possible to make the most unlikely connections. If you are offered the chance to work within another discipline or professional area for a short time, it could provide you with novel and exciting connections.

Use your experience

It is not only between disciplines that you can make connections; you also have a breadth of experience that you might overlook during your course. It is a good idea to undertake an 'experience audit' occasionally, making a conscious effort to work out whether any of your existing experiences could be useful within your studying. This might be practical experience, such as having run a professional workshop before or having given a presentation in the past. It might also be learning experience, such as having read around a subject in the past or having worked with a colleague on a project that could now be tailored to meet some of your course requirements. Although these connections are usually obvious in hindsight, students often have difficulty in recalling and reusing experiences at the best moment on their course: including an experience audit in your personalised timetable will ensure that you do not waste any of your experience as you face the challenges of a new learning situation.

▶ Keeping on track

You will by now have some basic records: your personalised timetable, your reading lists and your filing system of course materials. The usefulness of these records can be dramatically increased if, throughout your course, you keep two record keeping notebooks. These will ideally be hardback, A5 notebooks in which you will make a note of the books you intend to read and the research and assignment leads you have collected. You will note in your *reading notebook* each publication or piece of source material that you come across, and your various reading lists will be transferred into it as you personalise them, so that you have one, central record of the reading you hope to do in the course of your studying. If you include the full reference to each book, article or website (that is, title, author, title and details of full publication if it is an article, date and place of publication and publisher, website address and reference), this record book will be a blessing when you come to produce a bibliography.

The process is similar for your *research notebook*. Here the material will be more diverse, ranging from notes to yourself to look into an area in more detail, to ideas, facts and quotations for your next assignment and the beginnings of arguments you want to make. You will also include incidental comments that you have noted in preparation for specific assignments and 'alert notes', such as a warning that a piece of work has been discredited, or reminders (as in the manuscript comment in the website notes above) that you need to address an issue in your work. This book will be messy, which is all to the good. It is where you will begin the journey of working through your ideas, developing your own train of thought and exploring new areas of source material. As with your reading notebook, you will record the source of these notes, writing 'my idea' by those that are your own, and a tutor's name, website or text reference beside others. There will be some overlap between your reading and research notebooks, in that the publications of authors you mention in passing in your research notebook will be transferred to your reading notebooks once you have discovered the titles. This is not a static text: you will continue to add to it throughout your course and, as with your reading notebook, you will draw a line through each entry as you use it, so that you can keep track of how much of this vital material you are incorporating into your assignments or research project.

These notebooks are going to become fundamental to the management of your course for three reasons. Firstly, they will be your guarantee that you are in control of your work; when you are under pressure, you will reduce your stress levels considerably by knowing that texts and ideas are 'safe' in your notebooks, ready for use when the time comes. Secondly, they bring together all the sources you are offered and your assignment ideas and so eradicate confusion: they are your unique reference index. Thirdly, they allow you to spend time varying your study tasks. Having noted the details of each publication or assignment idea, leave a couple of lines blank. When you are too tired to look at yet another book, or are waiting for a publication to become available, you can spend a satisfying couple of hours noting the library references beneath each text or pondering the connections between your ideas and adding a few more notes. Within your reading notebook, when you have read the book or examined the source material, or perhaps glanced at it and discarded it (this will happen relatively often), you can then cross through the reference in your notebook to show that you have covered it, but you will still be able to see the full reference. Within your research notebook, you will be surprised to find that you have used some of the ideas and facts in assignments without even realising it, and you can spend this time crossing these through. You will soon be in a position to check back and feel the satisfaction of having completed a whole page of references and notes. Once you have done this, you can snip off the corner of that page, to indicate that it has been covered. This process is deliberately empowering: it will reduce your anxiety, remind you how much work you have done and show you at a glance how much is left to do.

Research tagging

In developing your research management techniques, you might consider producing a 'research sheet' for each area you are exploring or assignment you are preparing to write. One of the greatest dangers faced by distance and open learners is that of simply losing their way, forgetting texts they meant to look up for an assignment and overlooking areas of research they intended to explore whilst they try to keep up with the set tasks within their course. Avoiding this problem is relatively simple and becomes easier with practice. By entering the references and ideas for one piece of work from your research notebook onto an assignment research sheet you can isolate them, thus ensuring that you do not miss anything. You will begin to see the emerging shape of your plan, but you will be able to alter that plan in your mind as your work progresses. This allows you to work in two stages: a research sheet which develops as you carry out your research, work through your tutor packs and read your texts, followed in the later stages by a draft plan that you can assess and modify, perhaps discussing it with your tutor or supervisor, before producing a full plan.

In the example used earlier in this chapter, our student was working on an assessed essay entitled 'Women in waiting: seventeenth-century, female-authored publications'. She thinks this is a catchy title, but knows it will need some interpretation, so she begins her research sheet with an overview of what she is trying to say (this might change over time as she discusses her draft plan with her study partner and discussion group). She then pulls together research strands from her research notebook and notes down references from her reading notebooks.

Women in waiting: seventeenth-century, female-authored publications

INTRO

- not covering manuscript sources in much detail – just print publications
- history of print – problems of publication as somehow inappropriate for the nobility
- overview – publishing was a male-dominated activity in a patriarchal society and women had to wait in the wings, sneaking into publication where they could and using a male discourse to express themselves
  opening sentence? make it sound better – less definite and more of a hypothesis

PART ONE?

- talk about research challenges, including women publishing under initials
- talk about history of women and writing, in brief
  go back to the invention of the printing press
  look at Shenner's work on women and writing
  give example of T.C. and her 1640 poetry collection

CONC?

- maybe link problems of female-authored publications then and similar problems now? Are there any? Check back to 'women and writing' tutor pack notes
- were there any exceptions to the general categories of publication?
- any 'odd' publications that I could use as examples?
  include Mary Walters and the 1612 funeral sermon she wrote for herself on her deathbed
  check back to Dr Becker website notes and module three tutor pack and video lecture

PART TWO?

- why and how did women get published?
  - funeral sermons? *1630 collection as example*

PART THREE?

  - advice to children? *Lady Cavendish relevant enough?*
  - pious mediations? *don't forget to include male examples for comparison*
  - religious propaganda? *maybe have this as a section on its own?*
- give examples of women in print and show how these fit into different genres

This is clearly a research sheet rather than a developed plan; it allows our student to keep an open mind as she develops her research. The first research sheet she produces might not be this organised: it might be no more than a random jotting down of ideas and sources, aimed at capturing them on paper before she thinks about the structure at all. This revised sheet shows that she is beginning to think about the structure of her work, although this will change. In the next stage of planning she will probably decide that the 'part three' mentioned in this sheet has been superseded: she has already included all her examples in the earlier parts. You will notice that the marginal notes do not list the parts of the essay in order: as her ideas develop, she might alter these marginal notes to rearrange her material.

Throughout the research sheet she has listed publications she has taken from her reading notebooks (she will add more of these in time) and she has included ideas and tasks from her research notebook. She will leave plenty of space under each section of the notes, so she can add ideas as they come to her or include more notes from her reading and research notebooks. She will be using this research sheet as the basis of her work towards preparing the essay and so will study in detail the books she has mentioned and will follow up the references she has noted. She is likely to make at least one further research sheet, revising and sharpening her ideas as she works towards a final plan. When she has produced what seems to be the definitive research sheet, this can easily be developed into a plan for her assessed essay. She will include in the plan all the works she has finally decided will be included; she will make a note of which ideas are her original thoughts and which are drawn from other sources; she will also include some whole sentences or paragraphs that came to her as she made her research sheets, as these will help her to remain on track with her planned ideas.

In addition to these details, she will also, crucially, include a word count for each planned section of her essay. This word count might change as she writes, but if she has an initial word count written on her plan, she will not find herself in the demoralising position of finding that she has 'used up' all her allocated words in the first section of her essay and now has no words left for the next three sections. It is unlikely that she will be using too few words: distance and open learners rarely find themselves in this position.

The techniques suggested in this chapter can seem like hard work because you are being asked to juggle so many tasks at once, but if you keep updating your reading and research notebooks, you will be able to review where you are from time to time and draw together disparate ideas as you progress. This is especially important for distance and open learners. You are in the position of having to be the chief monitor of your progress and also having to keep all aspects of your course under control. Despite having created a personalised timetable and filling out research and reading notebooks, you can still unexpectedly begin to feel that you are no longer in control, that each task before you is becoming overwhelming. Producing research sheets for each assignment will allow you to see at a glance how each assessed element of your course is progressing, which will reduce the pressure on you.

Studying strategies

If you are to work at your most effective, you will need to discover the ways in which you work best. Reading techniques have already been mentioned, as has the need to dovetail your work, home and studying lives by using a personalised timetable. Beyond this, you will need to establish how the mechanisms of your studying life will work. This is an individual choice: some students work well in busy libraries, some need absolute silence; some students can work for hours at a stretch with very few breaks, some need frequent breaks in their routine if they are to remain focused. You will work out your best ways of working, sometimes with little conscious thought, but the following guidelines will give you a head start.

Pace your work

The fact that your work rate and studying efficiency will increase over time has already been discussed, but you can be more scientific in your approach to this development if you would find this motivating. Think of a task that you undertake regularly, working through material from a tutor pack, for example, and then assess how quickly you usually achieve it. You are likely to find that you have an optimum working time (say, half an hour) before you begin to work more slowly. If you make a note of how much you can achieve in the first half hour, then the second half hour and so on, you will be able to assess your optimum work time. This does not mean that you should only work for that amount of time but it does suggest that you could study more effectively if you changed tasks after that amount of time, and then returned to your original task after a while. This can be difficult to do at first, but if you have several tasks ahead of you at any point (your personalised timetable will help you to identify these), you will soon be able to develop this way of working.

Vary your contact time

You will have a range of contact points within your distance and open learning course: workshop and discussion sessions, internet study chat rooms, one-to-one sessions with your tutor or supervisor and less formalised working sessions with your fellow students or study partner. Each of these is useful, but they can all become time-consuming beyond their usefulness. If you prepare well for every type of contact time, you can maximise the benefits to you, and you can include this time within your personalised timetable, allocating a particular slot each week for a visit to the study chat room or attending a workshop session each month. If you are able to do this, you will minimise the risk of finding yourself either feeling isolated or stuck in a rut with your studying routine because you are only gaining support and ideas from one source.

How do you take in information?

We all vary in the ways in which we best take in information, and you will not have complete control over this aspect of your course. You might be given tutor packs, internet access, media broadcasts and videos to view, and all of these will be the basic tools in your studying. However, it is useful if you can analyse now how you work most productively: do you prefer to talk through ideas with others, or view demonstrations rather than reading about them? Do you find the internet easy to work with, or do you prefer to work with hard copy texts? Do you find viewing videos and broadcasts stimulating, or do they only really make sense to you once you have made notes on them and then worked through those? Once you have analysed the ways in which you best assimilate information, you will be able to tailor your personalised timetable accordingly, giving more weight to those studying methods that suit you best. We tend not to ask ourselves these questions in everyday life, so a little time spent analysing your response will help you to move forward.

How do you communicate most effectively?

As with assimilating information, we all have preferred methods of communicating our thoughts and ideas. You will be articulate in several forms, coping with the many challenges that face you within your studying, but this does not mean that there is no point in analysing your preferred methods of communication. If you have a preference for communicating in writing, needing time to think before you commit yourself to articulating your ideas to others, there is no need to abandon this natural preference now. Although you will involve yourself in various forms of communication, you can tailor your studying so that you communicate with your tutor and other students primarily through email, or prepare plans in advance of face-to-face meetings, so your thoughts are in order before you begin to discuss them.

Polishing your work

Students tend to work within two approaches. They either work to their highest possible standard at all times, or they work to a lower standard than they can achieve, usually because they have lost motivation or find that their time management is running away with them. You will inevitably find that at times you are working in a rather less perfectionist way than usual because of time pressure, but it makes sense to analyse the type of work you are being asked to do rather than letting the polishing of your work become a haphazard process. I have often been approached by students who have produced a disappointing piece of work and want to explain to me that they had a valid reason for underachieving, and that if I could only see the wonderful unassessed work they had done that week I would want to increase their grade. This is frustrating for both the student and the marker. In an ideal world you would be able to give your utmost to each task, but in reality you need to use your personalised timetable to assess what must be done to the highest standards you can achieve (assessed work, presentations, major research projects) and which tasks can be done to a slightly less exacting standard (making notes on minor texts, draft plans for work that will be amended later, preparing for one of a series of workshops sessions). During most weeks you will not have to think about this, but if you can asses tasks in this way in the weeks when you know you will be pushed for time, it will allow you to make the best of the available time. Work that can be tackled now in a less perfectionist way can always be revisited later, but you will have got your priorities right and your assessed work will not suffer as a result of a heavy workload.

Develop a skills action plan

The issue of widening your skills base will be discussed in the next chapter, but in terms of your most effective ways of working, it is worth pointing out here that a skills action plan can help to reduce the pressure on you and so help you to work more effectively. If you are anxious about one skill area (for example, if you know that your note taking skills are not as productive as they might be), this can have a disproportionately negative effect upon your work rate. Rather than simply getting on with the work, confident that you will improve and widen your skills base in an orderly way as your course progresses, you can waste time worrying about how far you have to go: this is never going to be an efficient way to work, and your personalised timetable, complete with skills goals, will help you to avoid this pitfall.

Levels of detail

Even when you are working to your highest standard, you will want to avoid wasting time and effort producing too much irrelevant detail. Whilst full-time students are sometimes corrected for their skimpy essays, distance and open learning students are more likely to produce far too much work for assessment, which can be a problem for both the marker and the student, who then has less time to work on the next project. There are three ways that you can avoid this happening to you. Firstly, read the instructions for each assessed project several times, and discuss them with other students if necessary, to make absolutely sure that you know what is expected of you. Secondly, work rigidly within the word count: it is your best guide to the expected level of detail. Lastly, make sure that you contact your tutor if you are confused about what you are doing. If you find that you have worked through one-third of your plan and are already near the limit of the word count, it would be counterproductive to struggle on and hope that nobody notices; it will also mean that you are in danger of cutting into time that should be spent on your next project. Instead, ask your tutor to review your plan to see where you have gone wrong, or work back through your plan again to see where you can condense your argument or remove some extraneous material (this can always be included in an appendix later).

Even if you are an experienced student you will not be able to adopt all these learning strategies and study management systems at the outset of your course: nobody will expect you to be able to do this. It is more a case of assessing each one in turn as you work through your course, analysing your methods and identifying areas in which you can improve. You will have time to do this: your course is a learning process in many different senses, and developing effective learning strategies is just one area where you will be transforming your approach over time.

▶ Your support systems

You will by now be aware of the need to develop productive working relationships with your course contacts, but there is a wider support structure available to you. Below are some checklists that you can use to ensure that you are making the most of each of these potential areas of support for your studying.

Workshop and discussion groups

To benefit fully from workshop and discussion groups, you might like to consider extending your time together beyond your scheduled sessions:

- meeting before or after workshops and discussion group sessions, particularly if you all have to travel some distance and so cannot meet frequently, will give you the chance to talk through the issues raised, help to reinforce your understanding and expand your ideas.
- you will not necessarily be given the email addresses of the other members of your groups, so make sure that you exchange addresses amongst yourselves.
- if you have to give a group presentation, or want to work with others as you rehearse for an individual presentation, look first to your workshop and discussion groups for presentation or revision partners.
- even if a discussion or workshop group is short-lived, you can make a positive effort to remain in contact in order to gain additional help in the future, even if you are not sure at the time how these other students might be able to help you.

Research teams

Your research team might be drawn from the professionals with whom your work, or might comprise other students on your course, but the essentials will remain the same:

- be clear not only about the task before you, but also about the wider objectives of the team, which may be purely academic or largely professional. If you are undertaking a work-based project, remaining aware that the agenda for others might be purely commercial will help you to work more effectively so that you all achieve your disparate goals.
- should you accept the task as it stands, are you clear about what is involved? Can you achieve the objective? Discuss any obvious area of difficulty in achieving the objective as early as possible, not only with your course providers but also with your research colleagues.
- is there a precedent for this work? Can you use the output or working methods of similar teams you have encountered, either within your course structure or your professional life?
- ensure that the whole team is aware of the plan as it develops and work assertively within the team, planning your timetable and playing to your strengths. Keep the lines of communication open: avoid excluding any member of the team.

- make sure that everyone involved in the team (and the wider academic world) is made aware of your success as the project draws to a close.

Group presentations

You might be asked to give a presentation as part of a team, perhaps a joint research presentation or a workshop presentation. Whatever the circumstances, there are several guidelines that will always apply:

- decide initially how much you can cover in the time available and then cut it down. There is a natural tendency to try to include too much material in a presentation; instead focus on a smaller area that you can handle well rather than taking on too much for the time available.
- allocate speaker positions early: it is not usually a good idea to put your least confident speaker first, unless you can get away with having that speaker simply introduce the group and then sit down to let the more confident speakers take over.
- be clear about the assessment system. You are most unlikely to be given individual marks for a team presentation; if you are to be marked as a team, you must work as a team.
- exchange email addresses or contact numbers and keep updating each other regularly on your progress.
- always leave time to rehearse as a group. An experienced assessor will know if a group has not spent time working through a presentation together, so it is essential that you rehearse as a team to polish your performance.
- be ready for last-minute disasters. If one member of your team fails to arrive on the day, you are unlikely to be given an alternative date on which to present. It is essential that you can give the presentation with one member missing, so make sure that you all know the presentation well enough to rework it at the last moment. Have backup visual aids so that the presentation can go ahead regardless of last-minute technical problems.

Peripheral support

As you work through the study process, there will be people around you who are not directly involved with your course, but who nevertheless offer vital financial, emotional or practical help. The importance of including your family and friends in your plans has already been discussed, but there are other supporters who you might come to rely upon at various points in your course and these can be divided into two broad categories:

- *networking support*: if you attend conferences, or take part in study or discussion groups, you will soon develop a network of academics who you may rarely meet in person, but with whom you can keep in touch by email. Never miss the opportunity to extend this support: a full email address book, with the details of the research interests of each member of the list noted down, can save you hours as you work through your research tasks and will prevent a feeling of isolation creeping up on you.
- *practical support*: although a level of practical help for your studying can be fundamental to the successful management of your course, it is easy to ignore the need to manage this help. If, for example, you need help with the cost of travelling, your employer or course provider may be able to help, as long as they are made aware of the situation as it arises. If you have to miss a day school or residential study weekend, make sure that you have made a firm, and reciprocal, arrangement with a colleague who is happy to share the notes with you and then find out whether you can make up for this lost time in some other way. Distance and open learners are sometimes embarrassed about coming forward and asking for help if they have missed one of these sessions, but your course providers will be in a position to support you as long as you make it clear that you could not avoid missing the event and are serious about making up the work.

Study partnerships

These have already been mentioned and it is vital that you recognise and foster this relationship. It will consist of only two or three of you, each of whom has found that you work well together and can be of great benefit to each other. These groups will not form for everyone, and you may find that the practicalities of your situation prevent you from forming such a partnership, but if you do discover that you work particularly well with another student, who is on your wavelength and approaches study situations in the same way as you, or in a way that complements your efforts, it is worth nurturing the relationship. Your course provider may have organised day schools or residential study schools as a key element in your learning experience, and this partnership will not replace these, but your study partnership can be just as important, as you can work alongside your partner in a less pressurised atmosphere and gain timely support as you need it. Although study partnerships can work to some extent via email, face-to-face contact will reinforce the relationship, even if you can only meet up occasionally. Your study partner might not be studying the same subject as you: it is more about a way of working than the course you are taking. It could be, for example, that you like to carry out your research in absolute quiet for long periods at a time, but prefer to have some company whilst you do it, or that you enjoy talking through the framework of an assignment before you commit a plan to paper. In both cases, having a study partner or couple who are studying a different subject from you can be a positive benefit. You will work quietly for a time and then take a break together, when you will either ignore the work you have done and give your minds a rest, or discuss your work. If you are preparing for an assignment, you can discuss the plan in outline terms, even if your study partners have no direct experience of your area of interest. If you ensure that the trade-off works and everyone involved gets the chance to talk, you can make this the most productive relationship you form during your course.

Supporting your learning experience in the most effective way possible will not happen overnight, but it will happen, to a lesser or greater extent, for every distance and open learner. The key to managing your course successfully is to approach all aspects of your learning in a methodical and proactive way, analysing your opportunities, strengths and support structures and then making a conscious decision to work towards maximising the benefits of your situation and your widening skills base as your course progresses.

Spot guide

The key points to remember from this chapter:

- mastering your reading lists will be the first stage in managing your learning
- categorise your reading material and use different reading strategies for each category
- maximise the value of your notes: keep their layout uniform and work towards becoming a proactive note taker
- connections are all around you: making them will depend on keeping up-to-date reading and research notebooks and using them as you approach each assignment or research task
- a studying partnership is a valuable support within your studying life: try to nurture this relationship wherever possible
- research sheets will keep you on track as you prepare for assignments
- a skills action plan can be fed into your personalised timetable, ensuring that all aspects of your learning experience are integrated
- grasp every opportunity to enhance your support systems by identifying and analysing both the challenges of your course and the different types of support that you are being offered

6 Skills Analysis and Course Assessment

Troubleshooting guide

Use this chapter for help if:

- you want to assess your skills base
- you are uncertain about how to relate your existing skills to your study challenges
- you intend to develop your essential and transferable skills in a systematic way
- you are unsure about how to succeed in your written assignments
- you are working towards a presentation
- you find that your ideas become muddled when you are under pressure
- you are struggling to come up with ideas for assignments or a research project
- you are anxious about the assessment processes on your course

Developing your skills base

As a distance and open learning student you are in a good position to consolidate and broaden your skills base. You already have a set of skills, many of which you have developed over time without giving it much thought, some of which you have made a conscious decision to develop through your course. You will also have skills that could be enhanced by your course, as long as you make plans to do this in a systematic way. Developing your skills base is a little like identifying your learning objectives: it will happen to some extent as a natural result of your course, but you can improve the outcome once you have learnt to manage the process.

In many ways, distance and open learners have an advantage in this respect over full contact students, who may not give so much thought to the skills they need on a daily basis in order to work through their courses. For you, self-discipline and motivation will be vital to your success and part of the process of developing these qualities will be an increasing understanding of the skills you are bringing to the task ahead of you. As each new challenge is placed before you, you will naturally assess whether you have the skills to meet it, and how you can develop those skills still further as you progress.

The problem for distance and open learners, particularly if they have been out of formal education for some time, is one of identifying, in a relatively formal way, the skills set they have already developed. This is partly because we tend to focus on tasks in life rather than skills. Let us take as an example a student who has worked for a year on a customer help desk prior to undertaking a distance and open learning course. At first glance this might have little to do with studying, but in fact once the skills of that job are analysed (prioritising a workload, negotiating with a variety of people, analysing and problem solving, providing feedback and working under pressure), it soon becomes clear that the student has already developed a range of skills that will be essential during a distance and open learning course. The same will apply to you, whether or not you have been studying recently. In some ways, it can be just as difficult for students who are used to site-based, full-time studying. They may assume that they can handle a distance and open learning course with relatively few problems, and this may be the case, but the differing skills required to move from an on-site course to a distance and open learning course must be identified if they are to make the most of this new opportunity. Skills that have been useful to them in the past may have to be developed and adapted so that they can be used to their maximum potential now.

I have already mentioned how useful it will be to you to undertake a 'skills audit' periodically during your course, so that you can continue to develop your skills base in the most effective way. At the beginning of your course, ideally before the formal studying has even begun, you could carry out a 'skills inventory' so as to gain a measure of your existing skills base before you begin to set targets for yourself. The reason why so much emphasis is placed here on your skills set is because the development of your skills will not only help within your course, it will also be an advantage as you move into other avenues after your course, not least because a recognised and clearly defined skills set is highly attractive to employers.

In your initial preparation there is no need to try to relate your skills to your course requirements. You will not know for certain what skills might be useful as your course progresses, so a thorough skills inventory, covering every skill you have, will provide the basis for further development. You will also be able to analyse more easily which skills you need to develop if you are not too tied in your thinking to the mechanics of your course. We all tend to be too modest about our abilities and achievements, and it can be quite difficult to translate everyday tasks into a skills set, so it is a good idea to undertake this exercise with several friends or family members. Take a large sheet of paper (even if, at this stage, you do not feel as if you have much to write down), put a line down the middle and list 'tasks' on one side and 'skills' on the other. The example below will help to get you started.

Task	**Skills**
Daily administration tasks	Organisation, prioritisation, IT skills, effective communication via email, managing work systems
Chairing meetings at local sports club	Communication, persuasion and negotiation, networking, leadership, planning and preparation
Answering customers' queries	Negotiation, understanding complex situations, analysing problems and finding solutions, articulating ideas
Fitting work around school times	Time management, prioritisation, multitasking, planning
Reporting customer feedback	Report writing, analysis of complex data, problem solving
Joining social book club	Reading effectively, discussion of ideas, clarity of thought, self-discipline and time management
Creating personal website	Advanced IT skills, commerical awareness, thinking creatively, problem solving

Your skills set will be more extensive than this, once you have worked through the process. You might be tempted, however, to dismiss some skills with the thought that 'everybody does these things, there is nothing special about me'. Try to avoid this: everyone does not have the same skills set that you have acquired, and skills that you take entirely for granted might present a real challenge to other people.

Of course, skills are not fully developed overnight. Whilst you might be aware that a particular task you have undertaken in the past required you to produce reports, you might also be conscious of the fact that you always struggled with this task, and tended to produce the report at the last minute and with little confidence in the layout of your ideas. This is where your skills development planning comes in. Once you have identified the skills that have already begun to develop, you will be ready to grade them. Leaving aside the tasks section in the table above, you can link the skills you have to the tasks you believe will be imposed by your course, and decide which skills you need to develop. At the conclusion of this exercise, your skills inventory will look something like the example below.

Study task	Skills	Rating
Reading lists	Prioritising	MEDIUM
Reading lists	Reading effectively	HIGH
Workshop sessions	Planning	LOW
Discussion groups	Articulating ideas	HIGH
Discussion groups	Communicating	HIGH
Producing assignments	Report writing	LOW
Self-assessment exercises	Self-discipline	MEDIUM
One-to-one sessions	Time management	MEDIUM

Again, your skills inventory will be longer and more detailed than this, but the principle will remain the same: that of identifying your strengths and weaknesses in the context of your distance and open learning course, based on your existing skills set. You will not be able to say with absolute certainty that your ratings are accurate: you might see yourself as a poor time manager, only to find that other students on your course are less well organised than you and that you encounter no serious timing problems. You will have some safeguards if you have others to help you, but you will have to be ready to amend your opinion of yourself as time moves on. One positive benefit of undertaking this exercise, beyond helping you to focus on your skills base, is that it forces you to take an overview of your course, analyse what is going to be asked of you and assess your ability to meet those demands.

One potentially negative effect of the exercise is that it can leave you feeling that there is an overwhelming amount of work to do if you are to develop your skills base to the level that your course requires. This is never going to be the case in reality, it is simply that you have highlighted those skills that you need to develop, whereas students taking a less proactive approach will be oblivious to the skills development that they will need if they are to manage their courses effectively.

The first thing to remember as you face this skills inventory is that you will not be able to perfect your skills instantly, and your course will not ask this of you. It is only natural that some tasks will be undertaken less efficiently in the early stages of your course as you take positive steps to enhance your skills. The second thing to remember is that skills are not developed in isolation: you are bringing your own personal qualities to this task. One personal quality has been mentioned in the table above (the self-discipline required to work through self-assessment exercises), but you will be able to identify many more of these, and you can use them to explain why you are so good at some of the tasks that you will be set. In Chapter 9 these personal qualities will be examined more fully, so that you can highlight them for potential employers, but here the focus will remain upon skills development, with an awareness that your personal qualities will have an impact upon this process.

The best way to work through the management of your skills development is to be methodical and assess your progress on a regular basis. The pattern of development will always be the same:

- Identify the skill that you intend to work on first. This might, for example, be report writing, if you have an early assignment that involves producing a report.
- Assess how you can improve on your existing skills base in this area. In this case, perhaps by working through the report writing online tutorial on your course website.
- Monitor your progress. Did you achieve a high mark in your report? Can you get feedback from your marker as to how effective your report layout was? Has your confidence increased?
- Decide whether to move on to the next skill area, or whether to undertake further work in this area. In this instance, you might decide to attend a study skills workshop, or arrange to produce a series of professional reports so that you can hone your skills still further.

Although the route to skills development in this example is relatively easy, in other cases it is more complex. You might be aware of a skill that you need to develop, but unsure as to how to go about this. You might also discover that you are developing skills you had no idea you would need, and so need to formalise what it is that you are doing. Students who are working face to face with their tutors on a regular basis have some advantages here: they are guided through the requirements of their course, often without being fully aware of the process, and experienced tutors are on hand to help them to develop their skills on a day-to-day basis. For distance and open learning students the situation can be more demanding. You have skills that need to be developed, but to a greater extent this process is in your own hands. It is for this reason that you need to formalise your skills development within your personalised timetable.

Let us take as an example a distance and open learning student who has had to plan her work to some extent within her professional life, but is aware that her planning skills require some development. She likes to be in control of life, so she tends to plan assignments very tightly at the outset, and suspects that she will overplan her whole course. She has had little experience in giving formal presentations, and was horrified to find that presentations are to form part of her course assessment process. She produces a skills development plan in the first instance.

Planning

Why do I need it?

- need to let my research develop freely
- need to be open to new ideas
- need to keep my course under control

Review skill experience

- how did I plan the charity campaign at work?
- what techniques work well for me in time management?

How can I develop it?

- produce a personalised timetable
- revise my personalised timetable each fortnight
- decide on the best planning method to use for my first assignment

Where do I go next?

Thinking creatively

Why do I need it?

- to broaden my area of research generally
- to make sure that I do not miss things
- to make my presentations more exciting

Review skill experience

- no ideas at all – help!

(continued)

How can I develop it?	• brainstorm with Mike for first assignment • read course pack with an eye to how ideas are ordered there
Where do I go next?	• *carry out a focus review each month* • *keep my research notebooks updated*

Presentation skills

Why do I need it?	• terrified of presentations • not sure that I will work well in discussion groups
Review skill experience	• do I present well at professional meetings? • what about my work in last course?
How can I develop it?	• get some practice – perhaps to friends? • plan and prepare at least a week in advance
Where do I go next?	• *work through online study skills workshop* • *volunteer to present my ideas formally at workshop at end of next month*

Reading more productively

Why do I need it?	• find it difficult to decide what to read • have too many books in my 'to read' pile • tend to overread in some areas; find some tutor packs too dense • never seem to catch up
Review skill experience	• my reading skills for the literature circle • reading at speed at work • I like reading!
How can I develop it?	• sort my reading material into categories • return books to the library if they are of little use • make a reading chart to view progress
Where do I go next?	• *get reading notebooks. Make sure each week that every text to be read is in a notebook and mark them off as I get through them*

Our student may choose to produce one of these inventories every few weeks, or she may use a separate sheet for each skill area and then add to it and revise it throughout her course. She will make sure that her skills targets and planned activities are included in her personalised timetable so that they cannot be overlooked, but they might usually be included in her 'wish time' section, as she might be too busy to work on them in depth in some weeks. Whichever method she chooses, it is worth analysing what each of the completed boxes is intended to achieve. By identifying the reasons behind her need to develop a skill ('Why do I need it?') she will be motivated to work on it: there is no point in just assuming that you need to develop every possible skill area without being clear about how it might help you in your course. These reasons will change over time and this box will help to keep you focused on the demands of your course.

By reviewing her existing strengths in each skill area ('Review skill experience') she will ensure that she does not waste any of her past experience. Although sometimes she will not be able to think of anything to put in this box (as in 'Thinking creatively' in this example), the space will allow her to add anything helpful as it occurs to her.

The suggestions in the 'How can I develop it?' section are calls to action. They are not vague ideas about what she would like to do in the future, but rather concrete plans that are achievable within her distance and open learning course structure. By working to a relatively short timescale here she can gauge how well she is progressing. Once she has worked on her first skill development area she can include more ambitious, long-term plans in this section.

This development plan is all about ticking the boxes, really feeling that you are getting somewhere because you can see that you have carried out your plans and moved forwards. However, it will not work for you if it remains static: it should be part of a cumulative process. The final box for each skill ('Where do I go next?') is therefore vital. This allows our student to develop her next skills inventory, within which she will record the results of the actions she had planned here and review what still needs to be done. As she becomes stronger in some areas, she might decide to include other skills on which she would like to work, always keeping in mind that this is a process of enrichment which will continue until the last day of her course, and beyond.

▶ Enhancing essential skills

Some of the skills that you will develop during your course will be unique to you and your circumstances and will depend upon your course and the opportunities available to you. However, there are some skills that are common to all distance and open learners, so guidance in the areas of effective planning, producing assignments, writing persuasively, presenting orally, organising ideas and problem solving is given here in order to help you to work effectively through the process of developing these skills.

Planning effectively

Planning effectively is perhaps less of a problem for many distance and open learners than for full-time students, as you would be unlikely to undertake a distance and open learning course unless you felt that you were capable of being reasonably organised and effective in your planning. The problem that tends to arise is that distance and open learners are asked, within a new learning environment, to plan tasks and assignments with which they are initially unfamiliar. Until you have worked through your first tutor pack you cannot know for certain how fast you can do this and still remain effective; until you have completed your first assignment you cannot be sure how long it will take. As you can see, this problem is largely self-correcting; you will come to know how long things take and you can plan accordingly, but you might still be left feeling that you are wasting time and energy because you are not planning your work as well as you might. At worst, this could leave you believing that you are always running behind in your course, so it is worth considering some planning strategies at the outset.

Plan thoroughly

Whatever you are producing as a distance and open learner, from a minor report to a major assignment, you can only work at your best if you plan for each aspect of your course. This may be a new concept for you: perhaps you are not a natural planner, and tend to rely more on inspiration at the time, or the pressure of a deadline, in order to get through your work. This approach is unlikely to work in the long term. This is partly a matter of practicalities: if you plan your work, you can time your workload, fitting it into the other commitments in your life, you can be sure to make the most of each learning opportunity and, most importantly, you can feel secure about how your work is developing. It is also a matter of confidence. Distance and open learners often express concern about the standard of their work and then feel that the feedback on their course is inadequate for their needs: are my grammar and spelling up to scratch? Why does this self-assessment test seem so much harder than the last? Why am I wasting time in discussion groups that do not really address my needs? In reality, their problems are actually being caused by poor planning. They are confused about the overall shape of a piece of work, so the execution of it on paper comes across in a more confused way. They know roughly what they want to say, but it sounds weak or unsupported because they have not planned how to test a hypothesis rigorously as they progress. They have spent so long working through their tutor pack in a disorganised way that their self-assessment test is hurried and poorly thought through. They have no time to prepare for a discussion group and so cannot get the most out of it.

Vary your planning methods

Your personalised timetable will be the cornerstone of your overall planning, but when it comes to specific tasks, such as writing up an assignment, you need to know about your preferred planning method. To do this you will need to think back to other occasions when you had to plan a task in detail. For a task such as preparing for a workshop, you will be able to apply the same methods you used in the past for other meetings (checking the list of delegates and making contact with them in advance, listing the issues you want to raise, planning your ideas on an index card ready to bring them up at the meeting, following up each meeting with email feedback and so on). For a written assignment, you might be able to draw upon your professional experience (producing a draft then a detailed plan before starting to write, indicating the word count on each section of the plan, leaving 24 hours after writing it before checking it through again and so on). You might also be able to think back to your earlier education (with GCSE coursework I always talked through my ideas with others, I always used a flow chart or mind mapping diagram in exams to help plan my answers and so on). Try to identify planning methods that have worked for you in the past: you will not want to abandon them now just because the situation is unfamiliar.

As well as relying upon your existing planning methods, continue to analyse how you might plan each aspect of your course. You will find new methods that work well for you and these should be valued and reused rather than forgotten. When it comes to carrying out a skills audit periodically throughout your course, you will be able to assess how well your different planning methods are working and then consciously adapt them to suit your developing requirements.

Remain flexible

Although I have suggested that you plan for each aspect of your course, you must remain flexible in your planning. A method of planning that has worked well for one task may need some adaptation for a different task, your timing may alter as tasks become more complex, and these changes must be taken into account. Plans should not be straitjackets, constraining your thoughts and controlling every word you write. Instead they should be enablers, keeping you on track as you move ahead, but open to adaptation and revision periodically. Once you have a plan in place, use it as you begin your writing, presentation preparation or research task, but revise it regularly.

Producing assignments

Producing assignments can be nerve-racking for most distance and open learners in the early stages of their courses. Working through a tutor pack or self-assessment test is one thing, producing a report or other written assignment is quite another. Having worked in relative isolation for several weeks, you can feel surprisingly vulnerable when you are asked to produce an assignment. There are ways to ensure that you feel more confident about this process and the skills that you will employ.

Check for precedent

If you are asked to produce a short report on your work to date, there is no need to assume that this has to be done in isolation. You will want to focus on your achievements, but worrying about layout, length and overall style may distract you from this essential purpose. If you are anxious, tackle the problem before you begin to write by discovering if there is a precedent that you can follow. Searching your course website for example assignments could produce results; course providers will often include specimen answers within the appendices of course packs. Although the title of an assignment might seem very different from your previous tasks, it may be that its format can be based on previous work that you have undertaken. It is better to email your tutor asking for help at this early stage than to produce the assignment in a state of confusion which will weaken your resolve and decrease your motivation.

Follow the guidelines

This sounds simplistic, but all students occasionally ignore the most basic guidelines. There are three main reasons for this. Firstly, they are so anxious about the task (often because they have not allowed themselves enough time to complete it) that they overlook even the simplest instructions. Secondly, they prefer to work with the familiar, and so produce reports and assignments in the format with which they are comfortable, even if this is not what is required by their course. Lastly, they simply assume that the guidelines do not apply to them because their case is so unique and their area of interest so specialised that they must work within their own guidelines rather than those attached to the course. None of these approaches will be successful: spending time working through the instructions you have been given and ensuring that you follow them exactly is always time well spent. You do not want your marker to be distracted by the fact that you have altered the course format for a report or exceeded the word count by 50 per cent.

Use self-assessment to guide you

Although you are now being asked to produce an assignment for external marking, many of the tasks you are undertaking within that assignment may not be very different from those within self-assessment. Distance and open learning students sometimes overlook this point and forget that self-assessment and external assessment are part of the same process. Before you plan your assignment, check back through your self-assessment work to see how it might help you in your current task.

Archive your work

Archiving your work is the most effective way of ensuring that your study programme runs smoothly; you can easily make connections between different aspects of your course and can reuse your newly acquired skills as your course progresses. Keep a hard copy of each piece of written work you produce during your course (this is usually more effective than relying on electronic copies, unless you are very adept at revising and analysing work on your computer screen). These will allow you to analyse your previous assignments in order to assess your progress, remind you of what worked well in terms of layout and ordering when you come to produce more work, and give you some core material that you can revisit and, if possible, adapt and reuse in future pieces of writing.

Writing persuasively

We are all used to committing our thoughts and arguments to paper, but writing in a persuasive academic style can be a new challenge for distance and open learning students. As with other tasks within your course, you will be able to draw upon your existing skills base to a large extent. Remember that, whatever you write, you will always be trying to persuade somebody of something, whether it is simply persuading them to agree with a particular argument, or persuading an assessor that you are working to the required standard. If you feel that there is still work to be done on your style in order to make it more persuasive, you do not need to wait until you are well advanced in your course; there are some points that you could consider straightaway.

Who are your readers?

This may seem like a simplistic question, but it is surprising how often writers, even experienced academic writers, forget to think of their readers. The writing process becomes all about you, what you want to say, what you know about a subject, and far too little about the readers, what they are expecting, what they want to know, how they might be persuaded. For your self-assessment tests the only reader of your work might be you, but in assignments you may have several readers. If you go on to produce articles for publication or conference papers, you will be reaching a wide readership and it is vital that you do all the necessary research on that readership. Is the journal highly specialised, appealing only to a narrow field of readers, or is it more general in nature? Will your conference paper be heard only on that occasion, or will it be distributed via the internet or perhaps even published, in which case you will be seeking to persuade a far more general readership of your point of view? Although publication and conference papers may be entirely beyond your ambitions at this stage, you cannot rule them out as a possibility, and if you intend to submit your work for publication, this should be done as early as possible, as publication is a very lengthy process. It can be reassuring to know that even such formal work will rely on the same principles as your first assignment.

How formal should you be?

Should you be highly formal in all that you write, incurring the risk that you might appear pompous or unwilling to accept advice and ideas? Or should you be a little less formal, with the danger that you might appear too casual, not rigorous enough in your standards and academic vetting? Experience and research are the solutions to this problem. You will get to know the tone that will suit each piece of writing and there should be clear guidelines and, perhaps, specimen answers to help you, particularly in the early stages of your course. If you are not sure about this aspect of your writing, your tutors will be able to guide you.

How will you persuade?

Obviously you will persuade by the force of your argument, the quality of your evidence and the passion shown in your writing for your subject, but beyond this there are simple techniques you can employ. Their usefulness will vary depending upon the writing you are producing, but in every case you will need to allow your reader plenty of space to 'breathe' whilst reading, so wide margins, double spacing and a roomy layout are essential. Readers need the 'white space' of breaks within the text in order to feel comfortable as they read. You should also avoid jargon, unless you are absolutely sure that your reader will be familiar with the terms you are using. You will 'signpost' your writing, by making it clear to the reader that there is a logical order to your arguments, which the reader will be led through without any unwelcome surprises. This might be done by including lists to show the points that you intend to cover, inserting a sentence or two at the end of a section in which you recap very briefly on what you have just written and ensuring that each new section of writing begins with a clear statement of what you intend to cover next. Finally, you need to get into the habit of 'listening' to your writing. Initially, this might mean going back to a piece of writing you produced some time ago and reading it aloud. You might feel a little awkward doing this at first, but it does produce results. As you read a section of writing, imagine that you are on stage, reading it aloud to a large audience. Slightly exaggerate the pauses and put some dramatic impact into what you are saying. You will be surprised at the results: suddenly your writing is no longer in your head, it is out in the open and far more reminiscent of how it will be received by a reader than how it appeared in your mind as you wrote it. As you read, ask yourself questions: does it sound strained or pompous? Are you bullying the readers into agreeing with you or leading them along a path with you? Are your sentences overly long or rambling, or are they too note-like in form? Do you sound confident or weak? Do your sentences keep the reader engaged? Does your paragraph structure allow the reader to 'escape' for a moment or two in order to consider what you are saying? Once you have developed the habit of reading aloud like this, you will find that you can read your writing on the page with a voice inside your head, as if you were reading it aloud, and you can pinpoint problems and overcome difficulties easily.

Use the help you are offered

You will not be expected to be a brilliantly persuasive and authoritative writer at the outset of your course. You will naturally come to rely on the guidelines you are given and any examples you are offered. Beyond this, it is worth following up any additional help you are offered, such as online or face-to-face study skills workshops that deal with assignment presentation and persuasive writing.

However persuasive your writing style, you will weaken your argument if you fail to check your written output as thoroughly as possible. Checking your work by reading through an entire project in one sitting is rarely the best way to identify problems and correct mistakes. Instead, you need to develop a checking strategy that will be productive. If you recognise differing aspects of the checking process, you can then check your work by tackling each separate aspect in turn. The spider diagram below demonstrates how this might be done.

As you can see from this plan, there are many different tasks to complete as you check your work. By varying your approach in this way you will reduce the likelihood of becoming bored and therefore ineffective in your checking.

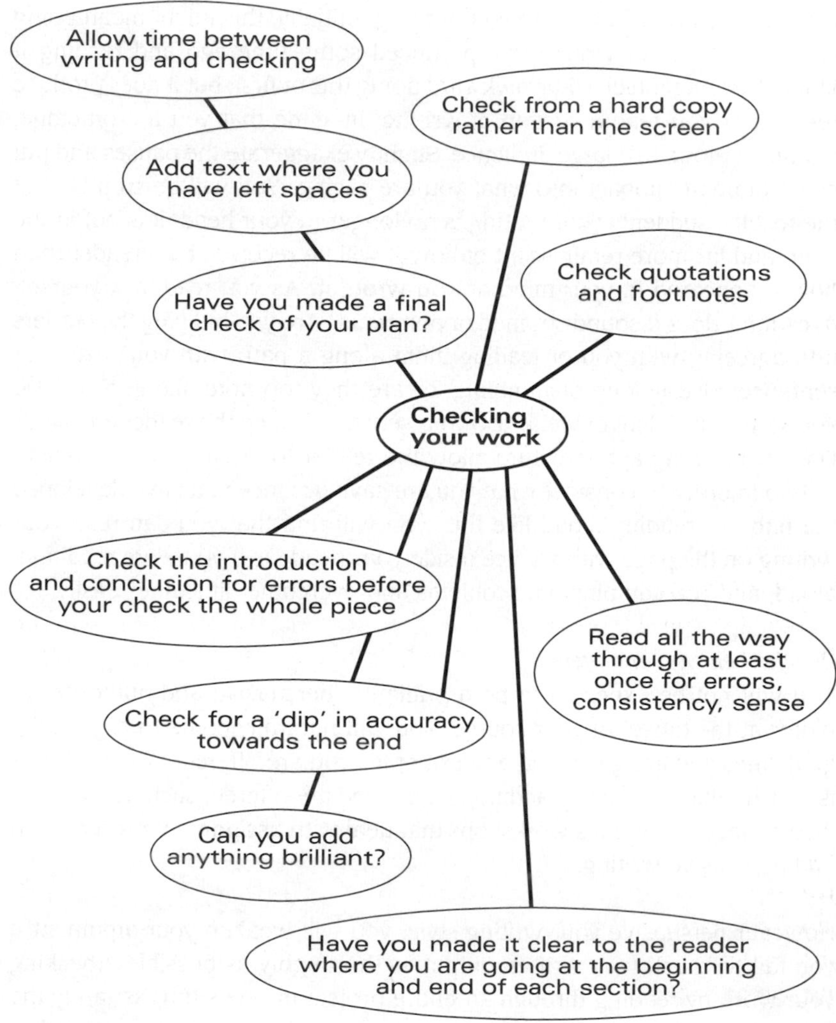

Figure 6.1 Spider diagram for checking work

Presenting your work orally

For some distance and open learners, presentations will form only a minor part of their studying experience: for others, presentations might form part of the assessment of their course. Even if you do not have to give formal presentations as part of your course, you might be asked to present your views as part of a workshop or discussion group, or during a residential study school or conference. If you know that you are likely to encounter problems with presentations, either formal presentations or as part of a discussion process, try these approaches now.

Assess your presentation experience

Can you increase your confidence by thinking back to a time when you had to give a presentation, even in a relatively informal way, to a small audience? If you can, then you are in a position to analyse the experience. What went well? What went less well? Where did your strengths lie? What comments did you receive after the presentation and can these be used to guide you now? For informal situations in which you will be asked to present your ideas orally, you will still be able to draw upon your past experience by considering how you react in meetings (Do you chair them? Do you contribute well? Do you find it difficult to speak up?) or social groups (Are you quieter than most of your friends? Do you lead the group?). This analysis of your experience will help you to assess whether you are likely to face problems in presenting your work now.

Practice makes perfect

As a distance and open learner you may not have the benefit of being able to attend group discussions regularly in order to develop this skill, but there are other ways that you could approach this area, and it is worth spending even a relatively short amount of time working on your presentation skills. Students on presentation skills courses are regularly amazed at how swiftly they can improve on their presentation skills, sometimes with very little specialist help. With even the most minimal level of help and support, you will find that practice is the secret of success. If you are not convinced, try giving a small presentation at home, perhaps just for five minutes or so. Make yourself practise it at least six times, leaving a short gap in between each practice. You will find that you are almost unrecognisably better, clearer, more measured and far more confident by the end of an hour.

Involve your supporters

This is one aspect of your course where you can include your family, friends and work colleagues in a positive way. Prepare a short presentation (perhaps just a few minutes' worth of material that you would like to present at a discussion group) and ask your supporters to listen to it, making comments on your performance. It is surprising how nervous you can feel even when surrounded by your family and friends, so this is a good test of how you will react in a more formal setting. Rather than relying upon their general comments (which are likely to be positive and encouraging, but vague), ask them to consider specific aspects of your presentation. Did your nervousness make you talk too fast at the beginning? Did you make enough eye contact? Did you make your main points clear? Were your points confused at any time? Did you finish strongly?

Use online help

Although you might not be able to practise your presentation with your fellow students, it can be useful to discuss the broad outline of your presentation with them by email. In this way they can offer you guidance and encouragement, and will hopefully have prepared some questions to ask when you come to give the presentation in front of them.

Organising your ideas

You will be coming to your distance and open learning course with a whole set of ideas already in place, either because your course is designed to develop your existing professional experience or you have a longstanding interest in your subject area. The challenge that you now face is to put these ideas in order, to test their validity and consolidate your opinions and arguments as you progress. You will not be expected to be expert in all aspects of your subject, instead you will be encouraged to develop your own theories, back these up with research and bring ideas and questions to each studying opportunity. Testing your ideas and articulating them with confidence and authority is going to be essential to your success in managing your course, and it is an area that causes more anxiety for distance and open learning students than almost any other. You will need to get the balance right: not just relying on vague ideas or anecdotal evidence from your past experience, but also not so weighed down with new facts and theories that you are unable to express any ideas of your own. At times you might feel isolated because you are learning at a distance, unable to test your ideas in an informal setting before you have to include them within an assignment. The process of self-assessment will help with this to some extent, but the best solution to the problem lies with learning to assess your ideas in a systematic way. There will be at least five different sorts of idea in your mind at any time during your course.

Received ideas

Building perhaps on your experience and your background reading, you will be gathering a set of received ideas within your field. This set comprises some ideas that are so widely acknowledged as to be in the public domain. If, for example, your area of study is criminology, you need not cite backup material every time you wish to discuss the unreliability of eyewitness accounts, as this knowledge is widely held and understood. It also includes ideas that may not be public knowledge, but are widely understood and accepted in your specialist field. In the given case of criminology, the idea that the reliability of eyewitness accounts decreases if the perpetrator of a crime was wearing the colour red is one such idea. You will assimilate these ideas with little conscious effort, but you do need to carry out a 'reliability check' on each section of your written work in the early checking stages. This is particularly true within professional development courses, as you might wrongly assume that your assumptions are more widely held than they are. Are the ideas or facts that you have presented really taken as entirely watertight by the academic community? Do you need to cite precedents or present evidence to support your statements? Should you pick apart a received idea in order to gain some research leverage, or should you accept it as a starting point?

Developing ideas

You will also be working with developing ideas, some of which may already have been forming before your course began and some of which will be new to you. You must be sure that you can differentiate between an idea you have worked on and for which you have evidence, and a discussion idea, one that is new to you and which you would like to work on as your course develops further. Some of your most fruitful work will arise from discussion ideas, so they are worth pursuing, but beware of the pitfall of relying on these before you have tested them. You will also need to remain aware that your tutor packs and any course material placed online may not necessarily consist wholly of received and established ideas. It would be sensible for course providers to include some developing ideas within this material, so that students are encouraged to think around the subject for themselves and either refute or modify the theories and ideas that are being presented, so do not assume that all the material that you are offered in this way is intended to be the last word within your subject.

Initial research ideas

You will also be grappling with your initial research ideas as you progress through your course. They can niggle at you for months before you feel in a position to explore them further, or they might be very much in the back of your mind until a new area of research reminds you of them. You will inevitably disregard some of these ideas in the end; indeed, you might cringe when you think of them once you have mastered your subject more fully. However, these ideas should be treated with respect: they are a sign that your grasp of your field is developing. They will provide you with many of the most inspirational points in your journey through your subject and they will enliven and inform your work, which is as much about asking questions as it is about finding answers.

Developed ideas

Your assignments will be made up of developed ideas, those ideas that you have worked through and subjected to rigorous academic thought and evidential testing. You will be relieved to know that this does not mean that every idea you include in your work must be absolutely without the possibility of refutation by others: academic life thrives on the proposing and subsequent testing of ideas. However, you must be able to distinguish between *developing* and *developed* ideas. You might, for example, choose to conclude an assignment with a set of ideas that you feel are raised by the issues you have covered, and this is a valid technique as long as your reader knows that you are not claiming these as any more than starting points for future work. The danger really arises when you become so single-minded about an idea, that it must be right and evidence must exist to support it somewhere, that you cannot resist including it and dressing it up in language suggesting that it is a developed rather than an developing idea.

Irrelevant ideas

You are interested in your field of study and committed to exploiting every scrap of knowledge that you possess, and so you will be besieged by irrelevant ideas, which can be both demoralising and disconcerting. In reality, the fact that some of your ideas will be irrelevant to your work should be taken as a good sign. It does not mean that the ideas are in themselves worthless, it simply means that they will not add substantially to the body of your work at this stage. They demonstrate that you are thinking creatively and laterally about your subject, so they should be welcomed as indicators of your lively intelligence, rather than being viewed as embarrassing dead ends. Irrelevant ideas are not a problem as long as you can spot them and not let them distract you. You will soon get into the habit of discarding such ideas when you need to.

Knowing that different sets of ideas exist for each distance and open learner only takes you some of the way towards utilising your ideas in the most effective way. When you reach the stage of planning an assignment, the advice given earlier in this chapter will help you as you move forward, but you can make the planning process even more effective if you use the flow chart below to prioritise your ideas within your planning.

Assignment plan

↓

Received ideas will allow you to set the context for your work and establish common ground with your reader

↓

Initial *research ideas* will show the direction in which your research has taken you. At this point you can demonstrate how and why you abandoned some of these ideas

↓

Developed ideas will be included here, to show how you have confirmed your ideas and answered your research questions as your work has progressed

↓

Some of your *developing ideas* will be included towards the end of your assignment, perhaps to show where you hope to go next or demonstrate your recognition that you have not answered every possible question within this area

↓

Irrelevant ideas will be weeded out as your plan progresses. Any stray ideas that have lingered within your assignment will be easy to spot at the checking stage and must be ruthlessly deleted

Creative problem solving

The issue of trying to find solutions to study problems is sometimes seen as a trial for distance and open learners, working in isolation and struggling with complex assignments. In fact, this is a misconception. Contrary to popular belief, full-time, on-site students do not necessarily spend their time sitting around talking creatively about their study problems, and distance and open learners often get the better deal here, because they take positive measures to put support systems in place. Working your way through the challenges of your course, aiming to remain open to new ideas and finding creative ways to solve study problems is the best reason for developing the support systems that were discussed in the previous chapter. You need to be in a position to draw upon a range of support at short notice when you are faced with a particularly thorny problem. There are three exercises that you can undertake so as to ensure that you continue to work through problems as creatively and productively as possible.

Online brainstorming

If you find yourself at a dead end, try online brainstorming. This technique can be adapted to differing situations, but in this context it would involve taking the key points of your problem (maybe the title of your assignment or the main elements in one aspect of your research problem) and listing them as single words or phrases in a 'round robin' email. You then ask your network of supporters and fellow students to add their ideas and suggestions to the list and, as importantly, their questions relating to the key points. Their thoughts do not have to be well focused, nor do they have to be directly relevant to the central problem, so friends who are not experts in your area can join in, and it is often a stray thought from a non-expert that will fire you up again. Once the email has completed its circuit, keep an open mind as you read through the results. Take each point in the email and think through whether it can be of use to you, perhaps by extending your current thinking about the assignment or research, or by showing you a quite different way forward. Often the most far-flung thoughts are of the greatest benefit in transporting you out of your dead end. Once you have set off on your new track, keep the brainstorming results for future reference, just in case you get stuck again.

Focus review

Every now and then (perhaps every month), carry out a focus review. This is not an onerous task, and need not take up much of your time. As you work your way through your course, you will be offered new ideas, shown new ways of looking at old issues and challenged to test and reassess your theories. These ideas will be included in your research notebook and from there they might be written on your research sheets for particular assignments. During your focus review you will work through your research notebooks, crossing out any ideas that you have discarded, ensuring that all relevant ideas have been included on your research sheets and reminding yourself of the ideas that you have previously considered but not yet developed. In this way you will not only keep yourself motivated, you will also be working towards each assignment in a manageable and productive way.

Details check

Along with your periodic focus review, you will need to carry out a details check on a regular basis, perhaps once a fortnight. This may sound boring, but in fact it is a satisfying and confidence boosting task. Think of it as an academic spring clean. You will have notes, lists of references to check and texts to look up, as well as half-completed pieces of work. To carry out a details check you simply work through your notes: are they in order? Is there any information that should be transferred to your reading list? Have you followed up on any ideas that are written in the margin? You then turn to your lists of references: do you need to order more books or work back over a previous section of a tutor pack? Have you kept up to date with your internet work? Are you really happy about missing out that detailed quote or piece of data simply because you will have to spend an hour hunting for it? Do you need to email a colleague to get a more accurate reference for a passing comment made at a study school? Your draft work in progress will also need a spring clean occasionally: have you made claims which really require some expansion to make your meaning clear? Have you made assumptions without bothering to back them up with evidence? Has your writing become too generalised, when a few detailed examples would make it more effective and persuasive? This is a pleasant task to do at the end of a busy week, but try not to be led astray into carrying out a whole series of new tasks: this is not the moment to rush off and spend three hours on the internet, or revise a whole section of your work; it is simply an opportunity to make a list of what you need to do next and make sure that all your various reading lists are up to date. You are not forcing yourself to be creative or necessarily think great new thoughts, but instead checking that everything is in the right place and that your work is as watertight as it can be at this stage.

Assessment

Much of the guidance offered in this and the previous chapter has been concerned with the practicalities of working towards assessment. However, in order to conquer the assessment on your course you will need to understand both the purposes and the structure of your assessment procedures. There is no point in spending too much time worrying needlessly about assessment if, in reality, only a small proportion of your output is to be assessed; equally, you will not want to overlook the assessment implications of any of your work. If you are to manage your course effectively, you will need to get to grips with assessment and to do this you must ask yourself, and your course providers, some fundamental questions.

How much of my work is being assessed?
This may seem like an odd question, but course providers do not always make clear which body of work is being assessed at each stage of the assessment process. You need to ask whether you are expected to demonstrate all your acquired knowledge to date in an assignment, for example, or whether its sphere of reference is much narrower. To some extent a word count will help to guide you here, but it is still a good idea to ask questions, particularly if your course is rigidly modular.

What is being assessed?
Again, a seemingly obvious question, but the answer is not always obvious to distance and open learning students. If, for example, you are being asked to write a report, will it be marked specifically on layout and presentation? If you are giving a presentation, are you being assessed on content alone, or your presentation skills? If an assessment exercise is divided into sections, have you been told how many marks are designated to each section? There is also the issue of 'getting it right'. You might assume that only 'right' answers will gain you credit, but in some cases you are being asked to explore a research methodology or question an assumption within your field and, in these instances, your methodology might be foregrounded for marking over your final answer.

What is the purpose of the assessment?
To some extent this question is linked to the one above, in that you can gauge what is being assessed (your written output, presentation skills, methodology) by how the marks are allocated. However, you need to understand the purpose of the assessment beyond these practical points. Is the assessment designed to discover whether you are able to move on to

the next stage of your course, or perhaps to help you to decide between future modules or assess whether you require further help in a specific area?

What will be the result of the assessment?

The result of each assessment is going to be vital to your approach and the overall management of each section of your course. It is frustrating to discover that an assessment you have slaved over is not going to count in any way towards the credits you need to pass your course; if you have worked on it to the detriment of other assessments, it might be disastrous. This is not to suggest that you will not work to the best of your ability for each assessment, but it makes sense to know in advance which assessments will count towards your overall course result. This can become quite complex as your course progresses: different grades might be required in order to proceed onto different stages of your course, overall averages might be weighted towards certain courses and the 'pass rate' might alter over different modules. Although you will not want to spend time worrying about every permutation within your course assessment, having a basic grasp of what is expected of you in each assessment phase will ensure that there are no unpleasant surprises waiting for you.

Can reassessment take place?

Distance and open learning students often hesitate to ask about the arrangements for retaking assessed tasks because they do not want to appear negative in their approach. Course providers will not see your question in this way. They are aware that you might be asked to submit to a multitude of assessments, from written assignments and assessment exercises, to examinations and presentations, as well as work-based studies. Each of these will be assessed in a different way, and you may not pass each assessment each time. This might not be a reflection of your abilities or learning, but rather the result of unexpected circumstances outside your studying, and understanding the possibilities for retaking assessments early on in your course will help to reassure you if you face a problem that might put your success temporarily in jeopardy.

What form will the assessment take?

This will vary from course to course, but forms of assessment on your course might include: electronic self-assessment tests; assesment exercises; research exercises; written assignments; work-based projects; a dissertation; presentations; and examinations.

Electronic self-assessment tests

- *What is involved*: these will be available to you frequently during your course, and are intended to allow you to work through your knowledge and skills base in a relatively informal way. You will be given the option of submitting your answers for assessment and then working through the process again. These tests may be based online, or available to you through CD-ROMs or interactive DVDs. If they are online, they may be monitored by your course providers as part of a continuous assessment process.
- *Advantages*: you can undertake the tests whenever it is convenient for you, and you can return to them repeatedly until you are sure that you have mastered an area. You can revisit them from time to time if you want to brush up on your knowledge base and reassure yourself of your progress. If they are not monitored, you can carry out the tests safe in the knowledge that nobody else will see your mistakes.
- *Potential disadvantages*: if you are working on a CD-ROM or DVD, each test can be slow to access. You also need to be aware of any monitoring of online tests. This will not be a problem, but it can be disconcerting to assume that you are working alone, only to find that your tutor is aware of your efforts.
- *How to make the most of them*: these can most usefully be seen as part of your preparation for other forms of assessment. Rather than working through them in mental isolation, assuming they have no relevance beyond your immediate activity, try to remain aware of how they might impact upon your other work: it can be useful to revisit a self-assessment test that you undertook some time ago as you prepare for a discussion group, for example, or to help you as you begin to think about planning an assignment.

Assessment exercises

- *What is involved*: these will take various forms, depending upon your course, but would include timed experimental work, hard copy tests set by tutors and work carried out in preparation for workshop and discussion groups. You might not expect these exercises to be part of the assessed work for your course, so you need to find out exactly what is and is not being assessed. If, for example, you have been asked to answer a simple questionnaire in advance of a discussion group, you might give it little thought, assuming that any gaps in your knowledge will be covered in the session, and it is frustrating to find that this work is being assessed.
- *Advantages*: these exercises are usually short and clearly explained.

They are not intended to be complex and are usually designed to test something specific (your knowledge base, most usually), so you can work within a fairly narrow remit and succeed.

- *Potential disadvantages*: if your course favours a system of continuous assessment, you might feel that these tests are getting in the way of your other study tasks. The only way to tackle this problem is to remind yourself of the value of the tests (they are usually an easy way to gain some credits) and incorporate them regularly into your personalised timetable, rather than letting them build up.
- *How to make the most of them*: because these exercises are designed to be user-friendly, there is no need for you to work hard to understand what is being asked of you. If you are confused, ask for clarification straightaway, as you will want to work through them regularly and at some speed, rather than spending too much time worrying about how to approach them. If you do not perform as well as you had expected in one of these exercises, make sure that you ask what went wrong, but then move on determinedly: there will be plenty more opportunities to prove your knowledge and abilities.

Research exercises

- *What is involved*: you will not be expected to be an expert in research at the outset of your course. Instead, your course providers will have designed exercises to help you towards the analytical approach that you will need to take as your research progresses. This will include undertaking basic research tasks such as critiquing published research and working through methodology exercises.
- *Advantages*: these exercises will be a fundamental tool for your development as a researcher, but they are sometimes assessed, so you must be clear about which exercises are solely for your benefit and which are intended to be incorporated into the assessment procedure of your course. Your approach will vary depending upon the circumstances: for assessed exercises you will obviously want to be as firm about your ideas and clear about your methodology as possible, and might work through established areas of your research and subject. For non-assessed exercises you can be more experimental, using the experience of your marker to guide you towards innovative methodologies and new areas of research.
- *Potential disadvantages*: once you have established whether each exercise is to be assessed or non-assessed, there are no disadvantages to these exercises, but bear in mind that any single methodological approach that is suggested to you will not be the only approach to take:

you will have to develop your own techniques and work with those approaches that best suit your area of interest.

- *How to make the most of them*: once you have established whether an exercise is to be assessed or not, you can draw on all the expertise around you to try out new ideas; it will not matter if you later discard them: this is the easiest way to establish whether your approaches will work.

Written assignments

- *What is involved*: these might range from short essays on a subject, reports on your work to date, to major written assignments that might extend to many thousands of words. In each of these cases you will be working to a deadline and, for some of these assignments, you might be discussing your work with your tutor once it has been marked.
- *Advantages*: the major advantage to written assignments is that they allow you to crystallise your knowledge in a formal way, articulate your arguments and become involved in discussions about your progress. They also allow you to mark your progress through a course: once you have completed a written assignment, you can file away some of your notes and tutor material before moving on to the next stage of your course.
- *Potential disadvantages*: many distance and open learners naturally find this form of assessment daunting in the early stages of their courses, particularly if they have not worked within formal education for some time. The advice offered throughout this book will help you to work through this form of assessment with minimal difficulty, but make sure that you sign up to any study skills courses you feel you need in advance of your first major written assignment.
- *How to make the most of them*: finding out how many marks on your course rely on each written assignment will help you to plan effectively for them. It is useful to see a written assignment as more than just one part of the assessment process: it is also a chance to discuss your ideas and arguments with the marker, either in person in a tutorial session or via email. Written assignments should never be discarded and forgotten once they have been marked. Archive the material and revisit it from time to time to see whether any of it can be reused, perhaps for a presentation or discussion group session.

Work-based projects

- *What is involved:* these are your chance to bring your professional life within the orbit of your course. They can be extensive, perhaps lasting several weeks, and they will be supervised by your course providers and, usually, a professional mentor.

- *Advantages:* they can make a nice break from purely academic work, as you can bring your existing professional expertise to the project and they can reduce the time pressure on you if you can carry out a project in your work time.
- *Potential disadvantages:* it can sometimes be difficult to ensure that all parties are agreed about what you are aiming to do. Your professional mentor or work colleagues might have a way of doing things that differs from your course provider's advice, or they may simply misunderstand your goals and so hinder your progress. You can avoid problems by keeping the lines of communication open from the outset of the project.
- *How to make the most of them:* be certain about the purpose of the project and the resources you need and make these clear to everyone involved in the planning stages so as to minimise problems later. Publicise your activities within your workplace so your colleagues know that you have a limited amount of time in which to complete the project, and you might therefore be less fully available than usual at certain points in that period.

A dissertation

- *What is involved*: this will be an extended piece of work (typically 15,000–20,000 words) that will allow you to range more widely within your subject area or develop your own lines of research. It will not necessarily require you to carry out original research, but it will necessitate a high level of independent work. A dissertation is often 'bolted on' to the end of a course and is carried out after the completion of the set modules.
- *Advantages:* producing a dissertation can be an exciting experience. It can help you to individualise your course, making it more relevant to your professional development, or allowing you to look in depth at an area of particular interest. It also gives you the opportunity to work on a one-to-one basis with your supervisor, who will offer you support as you progress.
- *Potential disadvantages:* it can be a lonely process, especially if you have completed the structured modules on your course. It can be a challenge to remain motivated when there are no regular deadlines, study schools or self-assessment tests.
- *How to make the most of it:* if you know that you might suffer from feeling isolated, make sure that you have put structures in place to support you as your dissertation progresses. Keep in touch with other

students who are writing dissertations and keep up regular contact with your supervisor. Producing a dissertation can stretch far beyond your original deadline if you are not careful, but undertaking many of the planning tasks in advance, whilst the structured part of your course is still running, can help you to get a head start in the process.

Presentations

- *What is involved*: you might be asked to give group or solo presentations and these can range from a 5-minute introduction to a discussion group to professional-level presentations of 30 minutes or more. They are sometimes assessed, both for content and presentation, and will usually represent the culmination of a period of study.
- *Advantages*: they can be a relatively easy way to gain some credits on your course, the preparation for them can be enjoyable and the material you include in them will be far less than you at first supposed.
- *Potential disadvantages*: if you are nervous about giving a presentation, or are not a natural presenter, they can be nerve-racking. The good news is that your course provider may provide study skills workshops for presentations, and if this is not the case, there are plenty of other opportunities to practise, both within your professional and social lives.
- *How to make the most of them*: follow the advice given earlier in this book and remember the key to success for all presentations: practice. Once you begin to practise you will find it easy to see where you can cut down on material if you are running over time, how you might be able to produce more effective visual aids and how you can use your voice and body language for greater impact.

Examinations

- *What is involved*: distance and open learning courses tend not to rely heavily on examinations, partly because of the practicalities of geography and partly because of the principles behind distance and open learning, such as the flexibility that these courses are designed to offer students in terms of their rate of progress and their means of demonstrating that progress. However, you may face examinations at some point, so it is worth checking with your course provider in the early stages whether this form of assessment will apply to you.
- *Advantages*: examinations offer you definite milestones in your course: the examination is over, so you can move on to the next stage and put that work behind you. They might also allow you to demonstrate your progress to an employer, who might be unfamiliar with more innovative means of assessment.

- *Potential disadvantages*: you might have chosen a distance and open learning course as a means of escaping from examinations, and it can then be a concern if you are faced with them. Never let this put you off a course, and try not to let the prospect of examinations loom too large over your studying. If you had problems with examinations in the past, get help as early as you can: your course provider may provide revision and examination technique workshops.
- *How to make the most of them*: if you found examinations difficult in the past, try not to let this experience put you off. The examinations for your current course may be quite different from your previous examinations, both in their structure and the ground they are covering. Find out the details as early as you can (how many credits are gained by examinations, how long they will be, how easy it is to retake, whether they are made up of essay or short answer questions and so on). If you feel that this might be an area of difficulty for you, get help as early as you can rather than leaving it until the last minute. Online study sites and study skills guides can help with examination techniques, your course providers will have past papers to show you and you should get the opportunity to practise during your course.

You will have seen in this chapter how developing your skills and preparing for assessment are integral elements within the learning process. I hope that you will see them in this way, rather than as separate tasks that have to be fitted into your personalised timetable somewhere. Timing might be a challenge for you in the early stages: you might leave too little time for your skills development plans and too much time for assessment preparation, but this will right itself as you become more experienced. The fundamental point is that these tasks do need to be included in your personalised timetable in a positive way, just as much as your reading, note taking and study schools. Whatever your subject, whatever the structure of your course, you will be able to develop your skills base, and you will come to see assessment as an affirmative element of your course, one in which you can succeed and so reinforce your learning experience.

Spot guide

The key points to remember from this chapter:

- you already have a valuable skills base that will be relevant to your studying needs
- an initial skills audit will help you to identify your strengths as you work towards developing your skills set
- incorporate your skills development plan into your personalised timetable
- set yourself specific skills targets and make realistic plans to achieve them
- planning thoroughly as you progress through your course will reduce your stress levels
- writing persuasively is largely a case of considering your reader, planning in detail and 'listening' to your writing
- your presentation skills will improve rapidly with a little practice
- arrange your ideas by category so that you can use them effectively
- online brainstorming is an easy way to overcome creative blocks as you produce an assignment
- be absolutely clear about the forms of assessment you will face and develop strategies for success

7 The Challenges of Communication

Troubleshooting guide

Use this chapter for help if:

- you find this new way of studying strange or intrusive
- you are not sure how to cope with telephone tutorials
- you find group sessions unproductive or overwhelming
- you are preparing for a day or residential study school
- you feel isolated in your studying
- you find the technology you need to access your course difficult to use
- you are not sure how to maximise your use of email
- chatting in a study site chat room makes you nervous
- you are studying in your second language

▶ Communication with your tutors

As a distance and open learner you are entering a new way of working. The experience will differ from your working relationship with past tutors at school, college or on campus-based courses, which can be to your benefit, once you have mastered the situation. The learning skills that you will develop on your course, discussed earlier in this book, will help you to move forward as an active learner: your relationship with your tutor needs to be an equally active and rewarding experience. The key is to refuse to see the situation in a negative light. Your tutor is there to facilitate your learning and will have to assess the development of your thought processes on the course, yet you will have limited face-to-face time with your tutor. You do, however, have a host of other means of communication which can be used to your advantage, even if sometimes the methods of tutoring seem unfamiliar, even intrusive, to you. You will not be alone if you find this new way of working strange at first, but taking positive steps at the outset of your course will ensure that the situation becomes familiar within a short space of time. The areas covered below are: telephone contact; group sessions; day school discussions, your developing learning skills; and reducing the sense of distance.

Telephone contact

For many campus-based students, the thought of talking on the telephone with their tutors would be most uncomfortable. We use the telephone to talk to friends or conduct business in a situation where we are sure of our role. Talking to a tutor by telephone differs from both these situations. There is a feeling of familiarity (we all talk on the telephone for so much of the time), yet also a sense that this is a relatively formal situation, in which you are talking to someone who might be assessing your response at every stage of the call. In practice, telephone tutoring tends either to be too short (with the student eager to get off the line before saying anything wrong) or too long (with the student desperately trying to make a point but finding it difficult to remain articulate). Neither of these situations is ideal, either for the student or the tutor. What you are both aiming for is a clear conversation during which you both know what is to be covered. Your tutor, having more experience of this, may take the lead here, but there are ways in which you can ensure that it works for you:

- *decide how often to speak on the telephone*: this may be an integral part of your course, if all students are expected to talk to their tutor each month, for example. However, in most cases the timing is up to you, and you will not want to either overburden your tutor or be uncommunicative, if this is a standard means of communication on your course. You will soon discover from your tutor or fellow students how often calls are usually made, but make sure that you speak as often as suits you, rather than feeling obliged to make a call if you really have nothing to say.
- *think about your reason for calling*: it is surprisingly easy, particularly if you are nervous, to make a call with a whole jumble of points that you want to make, and this is likely to be an unproductive call. As you prepare, remind yourself of the key reasons for the call. By doing this you will find that some of the queries could more easily be answered by email from your tutor or other support staff on your course; this will ensure that your call time is used to best effect.

- *check if it is a good time*: if you have not been given a set time to make contact with your tutor by telephone, always make sure that you ask if it is a good time to talk. Tutors are often reluctant to put students off by asking them to call back, afraid that the student will feel unsupported, but are happy to tell you, if you ask, that another time would be more convenient. In this way you can be sure that you are entering into a telephone call when you both have time to concentrate on the task ahead of you.
- *prepare for the call*: this is the key to successful telephone working. Before you make the call, write down the key points you want to cover and any queries you want to raise. If you are ringing principally to discuss a project, but have several other queries and concerns, you can work from your sheet of notes and say at the outset of the call that you have several other issues to discuss. Your tutor will then have a clear idea of how long the call is likely to take, and how complex the discussion might become, and your notes will keep you on track as the call progresses.
- *prepare your tutor for the call*: you might be surprised to discover that tutors can find telephone tutoring a challenge at times, especially if they are not naturally good on the telephone, or are unsure of the needs of the student to whom they are talking. If you email a list of points that you want to cover in advance of your call, this will help your tutor in preparing for the call. This will not be necessary if you are only anticipating a brief call covering simple issues, but is a good idea if your needs are more complex.
- *stick to your notes*: it is enormously frustrating to end a call to your tutor and then realise that you have forgotten to mention a point that might be important. You are then left to decide whether to call back, perhaps bothering your tutor with an apparently minor query, or ignore the difficulty until it becomes much larger. It will not be a problem for your tutor if you take a moment before the end of the call to check your notes so as to make sure that you have covered all your points. I am always impressed when students do this, as it is clear to me that they are organised in their approach to this method of tutorial.
- *back up the call if necessary*: although this will not always be necessary, always consider whether a call needs to be followed up by an email that outlines the details of the call, the publications that were mentioned and the deadlines that were agreed. This not only gives your tutor the chance to correct any errors in your interpretation, but also creates a permanent record of what you are both intending to do next.

Group sessions

The time that is available for talking face to face with your tutors is likely to be limited, so you will want to maximise this opportunity. Such sessions vary in their purpose and structure, but certain guidelines will be useful for them all:

- *be clear about the numbers involved in the session*: it is disconcerting to find yourself in a room with eight strangers when you had expected a session to run for just a couple of students. As your course progresses, these fellow students will cease to be strangers, but it is a still a good idea to confirm in advance how large the groups might be. If you have a two-hour session together but there are a dozen students involved, the individual attention that you can expect will be limited. This will not necessarily be a disadvantage: you can work with the group for that session and then arrange for further contact with the tutor if necessary, once you have had the chance to think further about the issues raised during the session.
- *understand the aims of the session*: it is rare for group sessions led by a tutor to be general in nature; this is the function of discussion groups. A group session will be held to discuss a specific project, to give a group of students the chance to discuss their assignments or to back up a module of the course, in which case the session might be like a lecture, but with some time for discussion. If you are unprepared for this, you could be left frustrated at the outcome, so be clear in advance as to what is being covered and how the session is to be run.
- *make notes on the points you want to cover*: as with a tutorial telephone call, you will get the most out of this experience if you prepare in advance, reading the notes the tutor has made on your assignment, perhaps, or making notes of a series of questions you want to ask about a project.
- *remain aware of the needs of the group*: if your tutor is expecting a general discussion about a project and you arrive armed with a long list of questions about your last assignment, much of the session will be spent with you trying to monopolise the tutor and the tutor trying not to engage too deeply in conversation with you. If it is clear, from the nature of the session and the number of students involved, that there is going to be little time for one-to-one supervision, abandon this idea and work with the group, supporting the general discussion and helping to move the group forward. This will inevitably benefit you, as ideas will arise and theories will be discussed that will be relevant to your work. You can reserve your detailed, individual queries for your telephone time with your tutor.

- *grasp this networking opportunity:* always exchange email addresses with every student you meet during your group sessions. The tutor will not necessarily do this for you, but the advantages of talking with other students by email cannot be overstated.
- *see this as the beginning of a process:* returning to solitary studying after a friendly and productive group session can be an anticlimax. This can be counteracted to a large extent if you work through your group session notes when next you come to study, highlighting points you would like to explore in more depth and noting queries you can raise with your fellow students by email. The positive effects of a group session can be felt for several weeks after the event if you take this approach.

Day school discussions

I have already suggested that discussions with tutors during day schools or residential study schools can be both limited and pressurised. This might result in you deciding against seeing this as an opportunity to gain some individual tuition, which might be the best approach to take, depending on the structure of the day and residential schools on your course. However, there are steps that you can take to open up the possibility of some additional tutorial support during these events:

- *student-run discussion groups*: if you are already involved in an online student discussion group or email network group, you might arrange to get together on the day (perhaps in a coffee break or during free sessions) to talk through some of the issues raised by your course. This will run well without a tutor being involved, but it would be a good idea to approach a tutor to ask if he or she would like to sit in on the session, not taking the lead, but contributing to the discussion from an informed and experienced perspective.
- *reading lists*: queries about reading lists are easily dealt with during day and residential schools, and it is advantageous to do this face to face because tutors tend to think of additional texts only when they are actually engaged in conversation with a student. Email your tutor in advance, asking for help with a reading list and arranging a time to meet up, with a clear undertaking that it will take no more than a few minutes.
- *extra time*: if you have travelled some distance to attend a day or residential school, it makes sense to consider spending an extra day at the university or college, which will allow you time to meet your tutors. You can arrange meeting times in advance, and use the time between meet-

ings to explore the campus, visit the library and resource centre and perhaps attend a lecture.

Your developing learning skills

An instinctive part of the life of every tutor is to assess the learning progress of students. This is easily done when they see the student on a day-to-day basis: they can pitch their teaching at the right level for the student, safe in the knowledge that they are supporting that student's learning outcomes in the most positive way. For tutors on distance and open learning courses the situation is not so clear-cut, or so instinctive. They may not see their student for weeks at a time, if at all, and so the question of how to pitch teaching at the same level as learning can become vexed. This potential difficulty can be overcome, as long as you are able to communicate effectively. There are several points to remember:

- *share your plans for development*: you will have been given a set of expected learning outcomes for your course, and you will have added your own target outcomes to this list, trying as much as possible to dovetail the two. As your course progresses you will be able to monitor your own learning and skills development, but it is vital that you share the details of this progress with your tutor. This involves sharing your skills development plan with your tutor on a regular basis, so that you are both clear about where you are now and how you hope to develop in the future to achieve your learning outcomes.
- *reduce your frustration*: you will inevitably find that some aspects of your course are pitched below your current level of knowledge and learning development. This is especially true of general study skills activities, but try not to feel so frustrated that you cease to be open to the opportunities that exist for you. If you are sitting in a session that is potentially frustrating, relax in the knowledge that you have already covered so much material and developed such a useful skills base, and then seize the chance to network with your colleagues over coffee and raise the few queries that are relevant to you. I recently met a full-time student who was abandoning university because she had to attend only five lectures a week. With so little time spent in the lecture theatre, she assured me, the course was clearly a waste of time. It had not occurred to her that the course offered her the chance to spend the other 35 hours a week working on her projects and developing her learning skills. Try not to fall into this trap: avoid the temptation to abandon a module of your course simply because the initial material seems too basic for you: the onus is on you to make

that material your own and use it to develop your learning skills and knowledge base.

- *ask for help*: if you share your learning outcomes and skills development plan with your tutor, you will be halfway towards your joint goal of maximising the usefulness and relevance of your course. The next step is to be specific about the help you need. This will be clear to you from your skills development plan, so it is an easy task to make it clear to your tutor by asking for help in specific areas. Your tutor will not mind if you reject suggestions that are made, as long as you can show your reasons for this and offer an alternative. If, for example, your course requires you to make a presentation and you have included this in your skills development plan, you might have made a series of presentations to your discussion group in preparation for the event. If your tutor then suggests that you might like to practise within a tutorial, you can explain that you have covered this area thoroughly, but you would like to spend some tutorial time working through the resources available in the university library, as you have problems accessing the resources online. In this way you can both be sure that you are spending your time together productively.

Reducing the sense of distance

This chapter began with the assurance that you will become familiar with the teaching and learning involved in your distance and open learning course relatively quickly. However, it is a good idea to monitor your sense of distance or isolation as you work through your course and take steps to overcome this feeling if it is having a negative effect on your studying. Many of the suggestions in this book will help you in this endeavour, and the checklist of activities below will remind you how to tackle this issue positively:

- *join a discussion group*: either online or in person, discussion groups ease the isolation that can result from distance and open learning studying, so organise your own group if this is not an intrinsic part of your course structure.
- *maintain your email network*: gathering email addresses is relatively easy on a distance and open learning course, but these addresses will sit unused in your online address book unless you take action. Each month or so, review your address list to see if there is any reason to re-establish contact with a 'lost' contact, or whether a discussion group might benefit from expansion.
- *organise your contact time effectively*: as the advice in this chapter has

suggested, thorough and clear-sighted preparation for all your contact time, with other students and your tutors, is the best way to make the most of this aspect of your course.

- *discover how best to keep up your tutorial contact*: telephone contact, email correspondence and online discussion groups will all supplement your face-to-face learning with your tutor. Try to see this process as an integral system, one in which you can take a leading role.
- *make the most of each opportunity*: it is, of course, possible to complete a distance and open learning course successfully with a minimal amount of contact. You might choose to restrict your communication with students and tutors only to that which is required as a course minimum. However, if you do want to range beyond this, view each aspect of your course, each learning situation and each point of contact as a chance to widen your experience, your contacts and your chances of communicating with those who can support you in your development.

Communication using technology

You will already be aware that technology plays a large part in delivering and facilitating distance and open learning courses. From online chat rooms and notice boards, to electronic assessment and email tutorials, this is an aspect of your course that it would be difficult to ignore. Whatever form the technology takes, you will want to overcome the obstacles that are common to many distance and open learners.

Becoming familiar with the technology

You will not be expected to be an expert in technology in order to complete your course, but it can be unnerving to realise that online communication is a key aspect of your course if you have never had much to do with computers and have no great interest in them. The most effective way to overcome this natural reluctance is to see technology as no more than a means to a desired end. Receiving instruction in this technology is relatively easy: so many centres exist for this purpose, both at your university or college and within the community at large. However, this is not the complete solution. The instruction that you receive will only really begin to take effect once you have used the technology, becoming familiar with the idea of logging onto your online system each day, checking your emails and visiting the course study sites regularly. Rather than thinking of the technology as a hurdle to be overcome, remind yourself *why* you are using it. You need to access course sites because the reading lists are lodged there rather than on hard copy. By checking your emails each day you will not miss out on events. Study discussion sites will allow you to find out what is going on for all your fellow students. Viewing the technology in this way will not eradicate all your reluctance overnight, but it will give you the incentive to persevere.

Increasing your access

At the outset of your course your use of technology might be limited to typing assignments and checking your emails. As part of your skills development plan, remind yourself to try out a new aspect of the technology on a fortnightly basis. This might involve accessing a new study site, or working through another module in your CD-ROM 'teach yourself' word processing package. It is frustrating to spend time laboriously carrying out a task (such as checking your word count or producing a table of contents) by hand, only to find that you could have achieved the same result in seconds on your computer. This alone will keep you motivated as your understanding and use of the technology increases.

Typing versus talking

Think about the process of typing as opposed to talking. When we speak we usually feel fairly relaxed about the process. If we make a mistake, we can correct ourselves, almost without thinking, in moments. If the person to whom we are talking starts to frown, we naturally respond to this, by either speaking more slowly or keeping quiet and allowing the other person to speak. Within email we do not receive any of these signals, and our instincts are therefore less useful to us. On the other hand, when talking we can say the wrong thing and feel embarrassed, or talk too much and miss the point of what is being said. Within email communication, we have time to think before we type, and we can consider the response thoroughly before we move on to the next part of the 'conversation'. Whether you prefer to talk or type will depend on the situation, your natural tendencies and whether you are communicating in your first or second language. It makes sense to analyse now whether you are naturally a 'talker' or a 'typer' and nuance your communication accordingly. You will not be able to dispense with either form of communication entirely, but you will be able to increase your use of email, the telephone or face-to-face sessions in order to favour your preferred method of communication, always bearing in mind the method preferred by your tutor and fellow students.

Public communication

When you first enter a study chat room you might feel uncomfortable. Is your tutor online and reading what you are writing? If you are receiving tutorial help in this way, is your response being assessed? Is the information you receive from other students on the site utterly reliable? The answer to all these questions is likely to be 'no'. You will probably be able to see from the 'site users' list whether your tutor is online, but most tutors will restrict their online contact to specific times and will have told their students when to expect them to be there. If you are talking through issues and queries with your tutor, rather than engaging in a test, there will not be any form of assessment taking place. Course chat rooms can become 'rumour rooms' from time to time, so you will need to confirm the information you find there with your tutors if it is an important issue. If you feel exposed, wondering who is reading your words as you type, or feel anxious about talking on an open site with your tutor, you can arrange to meet online in other ways. Your course organisers will be able to advise you on how to set up a separate chat room, or you can work with one of the 'instant messaging' systems that are available. If all this seems a little too technological for you, you can simply ask a contact on the site to email you direct, which gives you both privacy and the chance to think before you reply.

Maintaining communication

Having all this technology at your disposal is, on balance, a good thing, but maintaining it can be time-consuming and distracting. Be methodical about how you do this. Allow yourself two hours each week on the study chat site, for example, or include a reminder in your personalised timetable to update your email networks each month. Within this structure, reappraise the value of technology from time to time. A study chat room can be valuable at times, less so at others, so rather than developing a habit that becomes difficult to break, decide how much time to devote to each site and how much it is offering you. Having suggested that you monitor the value of technology, do not overlook the therapeutic value of some aspects of this tool. If you need a break from reading, checking your emails can be a pleasant and brief distraction. If you are in the middle of an assignment and lack the energy to continue, updating your reading and research notebooks with some online resource searching will ensure that you keep busy whilst you wait for inspiration to return. As long as you remain disciplined about returning to your tasks, you will come to see this as a positive and satisfying use of technology. The key to managing this aspect of your course is always to be clear about why you are using the technology, be methodical in your approach and firm about how long you are prepared to spend in this 'virtual' environment.

Communicating outside your first language

One of the benefits of a distance and open learning course is the way in which it allows you to study at your own pace in a second language. However, some distance and open learning students trying to keep up with every deadline of the course, despite the fact that they are also working to master their second language. This need not be the case: there will be structures in place to support you and you need to take advantage of these.

Analyse your communication skills

Recognising your level of fluency in your second language is the first step in this process. You may have undertaken an International English Language Test or worked through a language-based course prior to undertaking your current course, and it is a good idea to consider now which form of communication suits you best. You might, for example, feel relatively confident communicating by email, but find the telephone difficult (or impractically expensive if you are based outside the country in which the course tutors are based). Avoiding all forms of communication which you find more difficult would be a wasted opportunity, but you could plan much of your studying around your 'easiest' method of communication, reserving the more challenging communication for occasional use. Remember that your course providers will be familiar with this issue; many of their students will be working in their second language, so any problems you have will not be new to them.

Preparing to communicate

You will have noticed throughout this chapter that all distance and open learning students, working in any language, have to prepare to communicate if they are to be effective in conveying their needs and achievements. This is no different if you are working in your second language: preparation will increase your confidence and enhance your communication. If, for example, you are preparing to talk to your tutor on the telephone, you will have produced a list of points in advance, just as any student would do. Having done this, you also need to be ready to ask the tutor to wait whilst you check these notes during the conversation, and you might also have to ask whether you can call back later if you need more time to work through what has been said before moving on to the next stage. Communicating in your second language is tiring, and your tutor will take this into account and will be happy to arrange a series of shorter telephone calls to cover the ground if you would find this helpful. If you are preparing to communicate electronically, you will have the reassurance of knowing that you will have more time than you would have in a telephone call to consider what has been sent to you and respond. Try not to become so caught up in the potential for instant electronic communication (for example in a study chat room) that you then feel pressure to respond straightaway if, in fact, you need to take more time before you do so.

Face-to-face communication

If you have the chance to work in a discussion group or group tutorial session and find that most of the students are working in their first language, do not be put off. You might not always be able to keep up with the pace of conversation, but the event will still be useful to you. You will not want to spend the time saying nothing, so again make sure that you prepare something in advance, a question or a comment on your work that you can contribute to the session. No one will mind in the least if your language skills are not perfect; in fact, it is unlikely that anyone will notice this very much once you all begin to work together.

Developing your language skills base

It is exciting to be undertaking distance and open learning in your second language. Not only will you be studying in an area that interests you, you will also have the opportunity to improve your extended language skills as your course progresses. This might be a formal part of your studying programme, if language skills form part of the course structure, or you might be studying privately, perhaps by extending the pre-course study that you have already undertaken. If you are working on your language skills in this way, remember to set aside time for this within your personalised timetable. It is a task that will appear repeatedly on your personalised timetable, and you cannot afford too much compromise over the time you allow for it if you are to keep up the momentum for improvement.

Your fellow students

Even if you are studying language in a formal way throughout your course, you will find that your fellow students are in the best position to bring this process to life. People naturally tend to shy away from correcting other people's language. Unless they truly do not understand you, they will ignore any imprecision or mistakes. For much of the time this is the best way forward because it allows you to keep working on the task in hand, but it is a good idea for you to enlist the help of a few of your fellow students in your language development. They will be so impressed that you are working in your second language that asking for help in this way will not be a problem. Be specific about your needs, perhaps by asking them, when they have time, to correct your emails to them or listen out during a discussion group for any problems with your expressions. They will not pick up every problem, but this is a fast and effective way to improve your everyday language skills.

Your language skills base

As with any other skill that you are mastering as part of your course, include your language needs within your skills development plan, identifying opportunities for improvement and planning how you will go about this. Be precise about what you would like to achieve. A note simply to improve your language can be demoralising because it will be difficult to gauge your progress. Instead, target areas of communication (email, presentations, writing up assignments, talking in your discussion group) and work through them systematically, giving yourself specific tasks so that you can measure your success. If you make your tutor aware of your plans, you can be sure that you will receive the help you need at each stage of your skills development plan.

Support structures

For much of your course your language skills will not be an issue: you have shown that you can cope with a course in your second language and you will be focused on the tasks ahead of you. However, it is crucial that you find out about the support structures that are in place before a problem arises. You might, for example, be given extra time in examinations or for online assessment tests. If you are to give a presentation, it might be possible to team you up with another student so that you can work through the language issues raised by this challenge together. Your tutor can allow more time for your tutorial sessions. At day and residential study schools you could spend some time meeting with other students who share your first language, so that you can take a break together. If you find that your language improvement is progressing more slowly at times (this tends to happen as a natural part of language development), you might be given longer deadlines to work towards. If you feel isolated because of the language and cultural barriers you are encountering, there will be groups available for you to join; these groups might meet together or work only online, and they could be invaluable in supporting you on your course. You might not need to rely on any of these support structures, but it is reassuring to know at the outset that they exist and are there to help you, and if you encounter any problems, you will know where to turn straightaway.

Whether you are becoming accustomed to working in a new way with your tutor, struggling to cope with technology or mastering a new language, communication will remain an important aspect of your distance and open learning experience. You will not be able to perfect all aspects of communication overnight, but a methodical approach to the tasks you face, along with the determination to master this essential tool, will ensure that you manage your course effectively.

Spot guide

The key points to remember from this chapter:

- the working methods on your course will soon become familiar
- prepare for every telephone call with your tutor
- keep email contact relevant and specific
- group sessions need preparation and a willingness to support the group's work
- your tutor needs to know how your thinking processes and skills base are developing
- you can reduce a sense of distance on your course in a variety of practical, simple ways
- learning how to use the technology on your course is just the first step: you need to become familiar with as many of its uses as possible
- keep your network of contacts relevant by updating and using your online address books
- study chat rooms have advantages and disadvantages, but will always be worth visiting in the first instance
- you are not being assessed each time you access your course websites
- decide whether you are a 'talker' or a 'typer' and nuance your communication accordingly
- if you are studying in your second language, identify your preferred means of communication, widen your opportunities for development, include language development tasks in your personalised timetable and identify the support structures that exist in case you need them

8 What if Things go Wrong?

Troubleshooting guide

Use this chapter for help if:

- you cannot cope with the reading for your course
- you find e-learning difficult or suspect that you are not making the most of this opportunity
- you are disappointed in a mark that you have received for an assignment
- you are struggling to meet the deadlines on your course
- you cannot find the material that you need to complete an assignment
- you are worried that your course is not relevant enough to your professional situation
- you have not enjoyed a day school or residential study school
- you have given a presentation that did not go well
- you are unclear about the instructions that you have been given for an assignment
- you are worried about producing a dissertation
- you have ideas, but are not sure about how to order them
- you always seem to be running out of time
- you work hard, but never feel that you are on top of your course
- you feel isolated in your studying
- your course contacts are not helping you as much as you hoped they would
- you are disillusioned with your workshop or discussion group
- you are not enjoying your course

However well prepared and organised you are, unexpected problems can arise from time to time for any student. For distance and open learning students, the difficulty sometimes lies not only with the problem itself (which might be quite minor) but with their reaction to that problem. You might hesitate to ask questions about any area that is causing you a minor difficulty, and this can lead to the problem growing out of all proportion. If you suspect that a major problem is looming, there may be a natural temptation to ignore it in the hope that it will resolve itself: this can be disastrous.

The problems that distance and open learners might encounter can usefully be divided into two categories: specific problems and general problems. With the former, you will be able to pinpoint the difficulty but might be struggling to find a solution; with the latter, you are more likely to have a feeling that something is wrong but are unsure about the exact cause of your anxiety. Before looking at problems in detail, it is worth remembering that there are as many differing problems as there are students and you might not find your precise problem here, but this does not mean that it cannot be resolved or that it is not shared by other students: your course providers will have seen nearly every possible type of problem and will be able to help you work through yours. The sections below are starting points, so that you know that you have done everything possible yourself to resolve a problem before seeking further help.

Before you decide how best to approach your area of difficulty, you might find it useful to work through the table below.

Query	**How this might help**
How long has the problem existed?	If it is long term, it is likely to be a general rather than a specific problem, and might need some further analysis before it can be resolved.
Are other students encountering the same difficulty?	If this is the case, you will instantly feel less isolated and you can work together with your colleagues to find a solution; the problem might be with the course structure rather than with you personally.
Is this a recurring problem for you on this course?	If you keep encountering a similar problem, you will need to ask your tutor for help in finding the root cause of the difficulty. Problems with expressing your ideas, for example, can take several forms, but might all be resolved by one course of action.

(continued)

Can you analyse the details of the problem?	You might not be able to do this alone, but might consider working with a study partner to think through the details of your problem so that you can approach your tutor with a clear idea of what has gone wrong.
Can you relate your problem to your past experiences?	Now is a good time to think back to any difficulties you have had in earlier courses, or at school or college. Early problems have a way of hitting us again later if they are not resolved.
Is the problem likely to affect your overall course performance?	This may seem an odd question, but if you have a problem that is related to only one project, you might decide to live with it or overcome it only partially so that you can focus your time and energy on more productive areas of your course.

▶ Specific problems

Specific problems might not be difficult to identify, but they can be tricky to overcome. This is not because you lack the capabilities required to succeed in your course, but because different solutions work for different students. It can be disheartening to discuss your problem with a fellow student, only to be told that there is only one guaranteed method for solving the problem: a method you tried last week which did not help at all. Every student is different and will naturally find differing approaches to solving specific challenges, so I have suggested a range of approaches that you might take to solve some of these problems.

You cannot cope with the reading involved in your course

Feeling unable to cope with the reading is a relatively common, and usually temporary, problem, and often is not caused by the student at all, but by the way in which reading lists are compiled and used by course providers. The solution to this problem is usually straightforward:

- *Tackle your lists straightaway*: reading lists that are left lying about for weeks will always be a source of vague anxiety. When you receive a reading list, work through it briefly to analyse which books are essential and which are only to be used as backup material. This choice will depend on your level of expertise and the assignments you are preparing and might involve a trip to the library so that you can look at the books themselves before making a decision.

- *Get more details*: if you are given little guidance on which texts are of the most value to you, the simple solution is to decide how important they are by looking at them in the library, looking up their details on a catalogue system or emailing the relevant tutor. A vague question about the entire reading list will get you an equally vague answer, so ask for specific recommendations for your assignment or current area of study.
- *Think about the timescale:* although your reading lists might seem huge, if they are intended to last for your entire course, there is no need to worry: you will work through sections of them as the need arises. Ask whether these are the only lists that you will get and then work through them regularly (include this task in your personalised timetable) so that you can put only the most relevant texts at each stage in your reading notebook.
- *Develop reading strategies*: the advice offered in Chapter 4 will help you to develop strategies that will make your reading schedule manageable.
- *Update your reading notebook*: this is essential if you are to keep up with the reading demands placed upon you, but it is also a reassuring task. As you work through your reading notebook, crossing through those texts you have read and those you now know to be irrelevant to your needs, you will regain a feeling of control.

You find e-learning unproductive

Even the most experienced students can sometimes feel that they are not making the most of the technological delivery of their course, and there are several ways in which you can ensure that you are not one of them:

- *Spend time sampling what is on offer*: rather than allowing the IT within your course to faze you, set aside time at the outset of your studying to browse through the course website facilities. Force yourself to look at every IT opportunity, including chat rooms, e-tutorial sections, course information, email facilities and address lists. You will not want to linger too long in any one place, but you will gain an overview of the way in which IT is integrated into your course structure, even if you do not use all these facilities straightaway.
- *Pace your progress*: you cannot expect to be an expert in every aspect of e-learning straightaway. Sending your assignments in by email may seem odd at first, and communicating with your tutors via email or a study site chat room can feel stilted. You will get used to it, but try not to put too much pressure on yourself by expecting that it will all come naturally to you at the beginning of your course. Instead, decide if there are any areas of IT in which you need to develop your skills (perhaps

giving a presentation using a data projector or leading an online discussion group) and include these, one at a time, in your personalised timetable so that you give yourself the chance to develop these skills as you need them.

- *Use the help that is on offer*: your course provider should send you details of IT courses and online help facilities that are designed to support your learning, but there is no need to assume that this is the only help available to you. Training software packages can be useful if you prefer to work at your own pace and in your own time, but if you prefer face-to-face help you will find that a wide variety of IT courses are held at local schools, colleges and universities.
- *Aim to increase your IT interaction as your course develops*: it is tempting to learn how to handle a few key aspects of the IT components of your course and move no further forward. Your skills will be adequate for the tasks ahead of you, but you will be missing out on many advantages of the technology. Even if you have no specific IT skills listed in your skills development plan, make sure that you include time in your personalised timetable to take an overview of your IT interaction at regular intervals.

You have received a disappointing mark for an assignment

The way *not* to cope with a disappointing mark is to ignore it, however tempting it might be. It is understandable that you will feel some reluctance to work through the piece of work in detail with the marker, but this might be an integral part of your course structure. Even if this is not the case, you can only benefit from such advice, and you can reduce the awkwardness that you might feel in several ways.

- *Read through the work after a break*: when you receive a disappointing mark, your initial response might be to file the hard copy away or close down the computer after only a brief check through the comments that have been made. This is understandable, but after a day or so you must force yourself to work through the comments in a more systematic way, making sure that you understand what has been said and why the comments have been made.
- *Separate the particular from the general*: as you read through the comments on your work, try to analyse which comments are specific to the work (you have missed some material, you have not followed a particular instruction) and which are more general (your writing becomes confused, you are seriously under the word count). In this way you will understand why your mark was disappointing, what could be

put right easily and what general aspects of your work might need more attention. It is only in this way that you can decide whether this disappointing mark is just a temporary setback or the reflection of a more long-term challenge.

- *Note your questions*: once you have worked through the marked assignment you will be ready to talk to the marker in a more positive way. You will still be disappointed, of course, but you will be asking relevant questions. Vague questions from you might receive general answers: if you can ask about specific points, your marker will be able to help you in a far more productive way.
- *Maintain tutorial contact*: talking through an assessed piece of work at the time is useful; maintaining contact with the marker beyond this event is even more valuable to you, as it will allow you to draw on the marker's experience and expertise in future assignments. A simple email thanking the marker for the help you have been given and confirming the points that were made will eliminate any possibility for confusion and keep the lines of communication open between you.

Your course provider's deadlines seem unrealistic

The imposition of unrealistic deadlines happens more often than you might suppose: you are working through a course with few problems and then seem to be faced with a series of impossible deadlines. Your initial reaction is likely to be one of dismay and an insidious feeling that you are doing something wrong. Before you let the situation wear you down, consider these points:

- *Never assume that the fault is yours*: there can be times within any course when the tutors setting assignments simply fail to realise that they are being unrealistic. This is occasionally because a tutor is introducing an assignment for the first time and underestimates the work that it entails; it is more usually a case of tutors failing to communicate, so not realising that their deadlines clash with those for other assignments.
- *Keep the lines of communication open*: the easiest way to cope with this is to let everyone concerned know that there is a problem. If two deadlines clash, copy both assignment tutors into the email in which you express your concern about the time being allowed to complete the work. The chances are that you will receive a speedy response offering you the chance to extend one or both of the deadlines. At the very least, you will ensure that both tutors are aware for the future of the problems that clashes such as this can cause.
- *Rework your personalised timetable*: if your personalised timetable is as

detailed and flexible as it can be, you will be able to rework it to exclude all non-essential tasks for a couple of weeks whilst you tackle the assignments. Be firm about what is non-essential and try to exclude as much as possible so as to give yourself the chance to keep up to date. This will have no detrimental long-term effect on your progress, as the tasks will still be there, merely postponed. This is usually a more constructive way forward than simply determining to work through the night to complete an assignment. By amending your personalised timetable, you will be able to retain control of the situation and reduce the chances of panicking as the pressure increases.
- *Assess the situation upon completion*: reworking your personalised timetable to cope with this crisis is the first step; reassessing it once you have completed the assignments is equally vital. You may decide, once you have the time to assess it, that some of the tasks you had postponed have actually been completed as part of your assignment preparation, or can be reduced now that you have produced the main assignment for that module. You will not want to skimp on the work you do for your course, but equally there is no point in working for the sake of it: be as clear-sighted as you can and reassess your personalised timetable regularly so that you are in no danger of losing control of your learning.

You are finding it difficult to obtain material for your course
Obtaining the right material might not be a problem in your day-to-day studying, particularly if the material supplied by your course provider is extensive, but assignments often require a level of independent research, which can become a headache if your access to material is limited. Broadening your resource access will solve the problem:

- *Use tutorial guidance*: the reading lists and tutorial material you have been given are only a fraction of the resource material about which your tutor knows. If you have a problem getting hold of material, or find that it is not relevant enough to your needs at any stage, such as when you come to prepare an assignment, the first thing to do is to ask for more guidance. Spending some time browsing the internet will certainly give you access to material, but a few internet references from a tutor will help to focus your search and save you time. Working through journals for relevant articles can be time-consuming, and unnecessary if your tutor already knows of an article that will help you. This is never going to be a problem for your tutor, so do not be hesitant about asking for more guidance.

- *Assess your resources*: sometimes the problem lies not with too little material, but with material that you find uncongenial. If you find the internet difficult to work with in the early stages of your course, assess how much material you have in hard copy tutor packs and texts: there will probably be plenty for your needs at this stage. If you get stuck, spend some time browsing through your reading notebook for inspiration and looking through your archive material to see if you can reuse any material. Students overlook these resource opportunities surprisingly often, and they can save you hours of time.
- *Share resources*: one of the most important reasons for developing a network of colleagues and fellow students is to allow you to share information and resources. In general, students are delighted to 'give away' work that has become of little value to them. If you ask your discussion or workshop groups for help, you can expect to receive all sorts of material, from the notes that somebody took on a remote piece of research, to internet references that will suit your needs perfectly. Given the time constraints once you are preparing for an assignment, and the time pressure during discussion and workshop sessions, this is best done by a 'round robin' email as well as in person, so that people have the chance to think how best they can help you.
- *Ask for help*: as well as general requests for help in finding material, you will be in a position to ask for help in specific areas. Your personalised timetable will ensure that you are thinking about your assignments some time in advance, so you can ask for help early. This might include asking whether anyone has found the text that was mentioned only briefly in a discussion group, or whether your tutor or fellow students have taken copies of an article that has been taken out on long-term loan from the library, or downloaded an internet site that has mysteriously disappeared. Once you ask, you will not only be receiving immediate aid for your assignment preparation, you will also be opening up this possibility for your fellow students in the future, so it will be a positive move for everyone concerned.

You feel your course is irrelevant to your professional needs

Thinking that the course is irrelevant is not always obvious at the outset because the course literature cannot cover every eventuality. If you are beginning to feel that your course is not meeting your professional development needs, you will want to ask questions as soon as possible:

- *How much will this matter?* This may seem like a strange approach to take, but the value of your distance and open learning course will not lie solely with the way in which it impacts directly upon your professional life. Some of the most satisfying learning outcomes are the most unexpected, and developing your analytical skills and looking afresh at even tangential areas of study can feed into your professional approach in a positive way. Before you are tempted to abandon your course altogether, talk the situation through with both your professional mentor and your tutor, so that they can help you to see whether your course has a value beyond that which is obvious to you at the moment.

- *Is this a temporary problem?* Distance and open learning courses are designed to meet the needs of all their students, and you are likely to find yourself working through material at some point in your course that is less relevant to your professional needs than you might have hoped. This is all to the good if you can maintain a positive attitude: you are widening your knowledge base and still developing skills that will be beneficial to you in the future. As long as you can be sure that, once this module is completed, you will be returning to more familiar ground, this will not be a problem.
- *Can you customise your course?* If your dissatisfaction with the way that your course supports you professionally becomes a longer term issue, raise the possibility of customising your course with your professional mentor and tutor. This is an option for distance and open learners that is more common than you might suppose. Independent module options, supervised by a mentor and approved by your course provider, are a possibility. If you are undertaking a work-based project, you might be able to define your own learning parameters. If you choose to produce a dissertation as part of your course, this will give you plenty of chance to forge ahead in your own direction, which will increase the relevancy of your course substantially.
- *Do you have a mentor?* Whilst your course might not automatically provide you with a professional mentor, your tutor will probably be happy to work alongside a mentor. Your mentor's contact with your tutor might be minimal, but some dovetailing of the two relationships will be necessary. Ask within your workplace whether there is a senior colleague who would be happy to work in this capacity, or contact your professional body. This is not a one-way relationship: your mentor will enjoy the task and will gain from your experience, as you share your new ideas and discuss new approaches to your situation, so there is no need to feel that you are simply asking for a favour, and no reason to hesitate to ask for support in this way if you feel that it would help you to see the relevance of your course to your professional development.

You are disappointed in a day or residential school

Until you become used to attending day or residential schools, you might find that they do not live up to your expectations. This problem is usually resolved as you gain experience of working in this way, but you can take steps to ensure that it does not become a long-term problem:

- *Try to see this as an isolated problem*: it is common to feel a little deflated once a school is over and you return to your more normal pattern of studying, but if you have had a disappointing experience on a day or residential school, try not to let it impact adversely upon your whole approach to your course. This could create a huge problem from what is a relatively minor setback.
- *Do not assume that this will always be the case*: one disappointment is unlikely to be followed by another, as long as you work through the problem and make plans to improve the situation next time. It can be useful to contact your tutor after the event and express your concern: some emotional support and morale boosting from your tutor is a good idea at this stage.
- *Identify the problem*: there may be any number of reasons why you felt let down by a day or residential school, but the most common reasons are that students have unrealistic expectations of the material that can be covered in the time available, they expect more personal contact with the tutors or they feel socially isolated. You might also feel that you were left behind in the learning, which can happen if you are unused to working in such a pressurised way, or that your fellow students had a very different perspective on the course to your approach: this is unlikely to be a long-term problem once you have worked together for a time.
- *Plan to eradicate the problem next time*: it is only by identifying the specific problems that you can work towards ensuring that your next study school experience is a positive one. Some problems will be resolved by themselves: you will be more used to this way of working next time, more familiar with the material and have had more contact with your tutors. For other problems, you can take practical steps to overcome them. Contacting a group of your fellow students in advance of the next event to arrange to meet can help, keeping in contact by email after the event will help you to develop your networks, preparing thoroughly for the next school, reading all the material in advance and focusing on the tasks to be covered will guarantee that you feel more in command of the learning process next time.

You feel that you have failed in a presentation

Feeling that you have not presented as well as you might is rarely a failure. Unlike some other aspects of a distance and open learning course, presentations are a continual learning process: even the most experienced presenters are aware that there is always something new to learn, some new improvement to make. However, you will want to feel that you are moving towards that improvement as rapidly as possible:

- *Make notes after the event*: you will assume that you will always remember every moment of your presentation, but in fact you will forget the detail quite quickly. As you are given feedback, avoid the temptation to simply nod and smile politely; instead, make notes there and then and supplement them with your own reflections and suggestions for improvement as soon as possible after the event: you will find these notes invaluable when next you have to prepare a presentation.
- *Tackle one improvement at a time*: there is no need to feel that you have to become an expert overnight; trying to overcome every presenting weakness that you might have in one go will be counterproductive. Instead, choose one area for improvement, such as learning to breathe correctly, speaking more slowly or making more eye contact, and work with that improvement until you feel ready to move on to the next area.
- *Enlist help from family, friends and work colleagues*: your course might not give you as many opportunities as you need to give presentations, so this is a good chance to ask your supporters for help. Try giving the presentation again at home or work, with specific areas for improvement in mind. You will be familiar with the material and so can focus on your technique. This approach has the added advantage of drawing your supporters in a practical way into your learning process, which is a positive step to be making for its own sake. You might also consider increasing your presentation output by volunteering to give a presentation at a discussion group or within your professional or social life: practice really does effect improvements very quickly.
- *Develop relaxation techniques*: nerves will always be a necessary part of a good presentation, as they allow you to think more quickly and perform more effectively. However, allowing your nervousness to overwhelm you can be a real problem. If you are not intending to give a presentation for a while, you can still be working towards increasing your effectiveness by practising some relaxation exercises. There are a variety of techniques that you might choose to employ, and different approaches work for different people, so persevere until you find the methods that work best for you.

You are uncertain about the guidelines for an assignment

Despite all the efforts of your course contacts, not all instructions for assignments will be clear to every student, and if you are confused you can be sure that you are not alone. The problem that can arise in this situation is that the distance and open learner asks one course contact for clearer information, receives a vague or confusing answer and then feels embarrassed to ask anyone else for help. This is one of those problems that can overshadow your learning and yet is easy to resolve:

- *Return to the course literature*: at the outset of a distance and open learning course, students understandably cling to the course handbook and initial instruction packs as their only source of information. As their courses progress, these documents tend to work their way to the back of the filing system, but it is worth returning to this material occasionally, just to make sure that you have not missed anything. Students on most courses regularly look startled to find they have missed what to their tutor was an obvious set of instructions because it was buried in an instruction manual given to students months before.
- *Ask the administration staff*: as the administration staff on your course will be producing sets of instruction throughout your course, they are in a good position to point you towards any that you have missed. Beyond this, they can tell you the best person to talk to if you need a more detailed explanation of what is expected of you.
- *Check the course website*: you will become used to checking certain sections of your course website regularly, but tutors do not always notify students when certain key pages are changed. Web pages that deal with assignments will be set up before your course, but checking them regularly will ensure that you do not miss any changes that arise.
- *Do not give up*: you are undertaking a distance and open learning course in order to broaden your knowledge base, develop your learning skills and improve your qualifications. You are not on the course in order to be confused or undermined by worrying about unclear instructions. Producing an assignment with only a vague idea of what is expected is demoralising and, potentially, catastrophic. There is help available and you must persist until you receive it.

You are not sure whether you can produce a successful dissertation

Even if you are expecting to produce a dissertation as part of your course, it can become a daunting prospect as the time to work on it draws nearer. You will be able to succeed in producing a satisfactory dissertation and there will be plenty of support available, but some early reassurance can help to reduce your anxiety levels, which might otherwise adversely affect other aspects of your course:

- *Allow your skills to develop*: you would not expect to be able to produce a dissertation within the first few weeks of your course, and nobody would expect this of you. Although you may not be able to imagine producing a dissertation of 20,000 words or so when you are struggling with your first assignment, this is perfectly normal and does not mean that you will have a problem in the future. If your dissertation is in the later stages of your course, or an additional option at the end of your course, do not allow your initial learning challenges to put you off this possibility. Instead, gather potential material for your dissertation and include it on a research sheet, but ignore the mechanics of producing the dissertation until later in your course.
- *Be open to new ideas*: it is not generally a good idea to approach any studying with a fixed idea of how you will proceed in every detail. You may well begin your course with an idea of the subject area that you would like to cover in your dissertation, but remaining open to new possibilities will ensure that you end up with the most interesting and successful dissertation that you can produce.
- *Be clear about the support structures*: you may not need extensive support for your studying until you reach your dissertation, or you may find the support patchy in places. It is worth remembering that when you are about to produce your dissertation, a new support system will probably be put in place. You will have a supervisor to guide you through the process, and you will need to work on this relationship in the ways I have already suggested, so that you are clear about the level and type of support that you can expect.
- *View your dissertation as a developing process*: once you begin to work towards your dissertation, you might naturally tend towards trying to control each aspect of the dissertation, with a complex plan and word count system in place in the first week and your conclusions planned even before you have planned your introduction. Although you will not want to lose your way, and need to retain a level of control over the process, a close relationship with your supervisor will allow you to think widely and develop your ideas and research skills as the dissertation develops without losing your way, which usually increases both the value of the process and the quality of the outcome.

General problems

Some of the problems that you might encounter will be more general in nature: even if you can identify a broad area of difficulty, you might struggle to pinpoint the exact cause of the problem. General problems can have a serious negative effect on your learning progress, yet they are not necessarily more difficult to solve than specific difficulties once you have identified their cause. What is different about them is that you need to identify them as early as possible, as soon as you begin to feel unhappy with your studying life, and then take action. This need not be drastic action; sometimes just talking through the situation with your tutor is enough. In addition to this, there are practical suggestions below that will help you to work towards a solution as soon as you become aware of a potential problem. The description of the problem given here might not perfectly match your difficulty, but it will still contain relevant ideas that you can try.

You find it difficult to order your ideas

You will inevitably face some level of confusion in ordering your ideas at the outset of your course, particularly if you are new to distance and open learning or are studying in a field with which you are unfamiliar. Accepting this as a normal part of a new learning process will help you to cope, and there are positive steps that you can take to minimise the confusion speedily:

- *Maintain your filing system*: from the outset, your filing system will allow you to keep your course material in order; it is surprising how confused your thoughts can become if this system becomes either muddled or neglected. Although you may sometimes feel as if you are wasting valuable learning time when you are filing away your notes and tutorial material, in fact you are helping to put your thoughts in order. It is a good idea to maintain two sets of files, one labelled 'active' and one 'archive', so that you can gauge at a glance how much work you still have to do on a module or assignment and how much you have already achieved.
- *Review your research and assignment sheets*: neglected research and assignment sheets become more of a hindrance than a help. If you decide to use this method to prepare your assessed work, ensure that a regular review of all your current sheets is included in your personalised timetable. An hour spent reviewing and updating them will renew your feeling of control, an important aspect of managing your course.

- *Build in some time away from studying*: although you may not have the time to take a week or two off at any point in your course, it is only by forcing yourself to take a structured and planned break occasionally that you can give yourself the chance to ponder the ideas on your course in a less pressurised way. This may be no more than including a weekend off with your family within your personalised timetable, but by planning for it you will eradicate the vaguely guilty feeling that you can get when you take unplanned time away from studying.
- *Use discussion groups wisely*: if discussion groups (either face to face or via email) form a regular part of your course structure, make sure that you are getting the most out of them. This will involve planning for each session and following it up by ordering your notes or feeding back your thoughts to your fellow students via email. These are usually positive things to do, but if you feel confused or are under pressure to produce some assessed work, make a decision about whether to become involved in the next session. For some students at some times, a discussion group can provide reassurance and help with the thought processes that the student is working through; at other times the group can represent a distraction from more pressing tasks, entailing more work with little return.

You are running out of time

Running out of time will require both urgent and long-term planning. You will want to undertake some crisis management to help you through the immediate problem, and then put in place long-term strategies so that it does not happen again. Asking yourself these questions will help.

- *Do you really have a problem?* This may sound perverse (of course I have a problem, you might say, that is why I am reading this section) but in fact there will be periods when you are genuinely, but temporarily, running short of time simply because your course (and perhaps your other commitments) are causing you this problem. If you analyse the situation and decide that this is the case, you need do nothing more than work through the immediate crisis as best you can, safe in the knowledge that it is unlikely to be a problem that you will face frequently.
- *How can you solve today's crisis?* Whether your analysis of the situation reveals that you have a long-term problem or not, you still have to solve the timing crisis that you are facing now. There are three ways to do this. Firstly, prioritise your work and resolutely reschedule less pressing tasks within your personalised timetable. Secondly, enlist the help of

family and colleagues in any way you can, perhaps by temporarily taking time out from family commitments to study for longer hours, or asking work colleagues to help with some of the preparation for a work-based project. Thirdly, make firm decisions and stick to them. If you have decided that you simply cannot complete a piece of assessed work on time, for example, contact your course providers straightaway and let them know that your work will be late. By doing this they will realise that you are as organised as you can be, rather than having a last-minute panic, and you can reduce the pressure you are working under.

- *What will help in future?* If a temporary timing problem is no more than the result of situations over which you have little control, there is no need to implement new timing strategies for the future. If, on the other hand, you know that you have long-term problems, you will need to take action. These problems might include, for example, taking too long to work through reading material, spending hours browsing on the internet to little effect or hesitating for days before beginning to write an assignment. Once you have identified a problem, include it within your skills development plan (increased reading productivity, better use of technology, planning assignments earlier, for example). In this way you can ease the immediate pressure on yourself by knowing that you will overcome these difficulties as you work through your personalised timetable.
- *How can you monitor your progress?* As with all skills development, you do not want to wait for another crisis before you realise that you still have a problem. This is why it is so important to review your skills inventory and development plans regularly. If you do this, and then find yourself in another crisis in the months to come, you can be sure that the problem is external rather than of your own making. You will still have to go through the process of analysing the situation and rescheduling your work again, but you will do this with the reasonable certainty that the problem is not serious in the long term.

You always seem to be working and never catch up

To some extent, feeling as though you are working but never catching up is an inevitable part of the process of working within distance and open learning; indeed, it is part of the life pattern of any student. There will always be more reading to do, new references to look up and assignments lurking on the horizon. The key is to know whether what you are feeling is a natural part of the learning process or something more problematic:

- *Have you always felt this way?* The feeling that things are getting beyond you can strike suddenly, and it is easy to overlook the fact that you have always worked hard and under pressure. What might be different is not that you are getting behind or working any less productively, but other factors are affecting how you feel about your course. Are you just tired? (This can creep up on you unexpectedly.) Have you just begun a new, more advanced module? (Your studying life will settle down once you are used to the new study regime.) Is your professional life encroaching upon your study time? (This might ease, and you can consider a study break if you know that this will be the case after a few weeks.) Has your home life recently become more hectic? (If you have just moved house or cared for a sick child, these transitory problems will pass.) These seem like obvious questions but distance and open learning students tend to overlook them; by asking them it is possible to identify whether it is the course that is giving you a problem or other factors that can be solved without abandoning your studying.

- *Is your learning efficiency increasing?* One way to ascertain whether the problem is long term or temporary, and perhaps not caused by your course at all, is to assess your learning efficiency. I have already suggested that you check on how your skills in reading, note taking and writing are improving, and this will show you that the problem is either temporary, perhaps unconnected to your course, or more fundamental, in which case you can use your skills development plan and your personalised timetable to resolve the problem over time. Although this will not solve your immediate difficulties, it will ensure that you replace that vague feeling of unease with a positive plan of action.
- *Does your course suit your circumstances?* If you are beginning to feel that you have always struggled with your course, it is better to take stock of the situation than continue in a negative way, with the risk that this might put you off studying altogether. You may not initially have worked through all the factors outlined in the first chapters of this book in order to analyse whether you are enrolled on the right distance and open learning course. Now is the time to do this, taking into account not only your interests and professional needs, but also the ways in which you work best and the regular demands that your course is placing upon you. There is such a wide variety of distance and open learning courses on offer that, if you do decide that your course is not best suited to your needs, you can be sure you will find one that is. However, it would be counterproductive simply to abandon your course at this stage: instead, talk to your course providers to see if you can transfer your credits to another course that they run, one more suited to your circumstances.
- *Is your personalised timetable helping you enough?* A personalised timetable should be a positive management tool rather than a burden.

If you begin to see it as a hard taskmaster, with a never-ending series of tasks, it is a good idea to assess and revise it rather than simply working harder in the hope that you can catch up. Your course might not be the problem; it could be that you are working in an ineffectual way in just one area, or giving yourself too many tasks within the time available. If you have checked your learning efficiency and know that you have a problem with one aspect of your studying, such as reading and making notes, consider allowing time within your personalised timetable to work exclusively on that aspect of your course, by introducing a 'reading week', that allows you to do nothing but catch up on the reading and note making. If you are overburdened with tasks, decide now what you can sensibly cut out of your timetable: you can always reschedule the work later, once you have had a chance to relax a little and catch your breath.

You feel isolated

Although feeling isolated is a relatively common experience for distance and open learners, it is not always prolonged and there are simple steps that you can take to eradicate it:

- *Use discussion and workshop groups*: distance and open learning students are not unique in feeling isolated occasionally: full contact students also feel like this at times. For them, working within seminar groups on a regular basis can help, and for you the same applies to discussion and workshop groups. The sessions you spend with these groups, either online or in person, are designed to extend your knowledge base and offer you a forum in which to try out new ideas. Just as importantly, they are intended to help you to feel part of your course and gain the support of your fellow students. If you feel isolated, take advantage of every discussion and workshop group available to you, even if the subjects under discussion are not directly related to your current course tasks. As long as this does not impact too greatly on your personalised timetable, it may be time well spent.
- *Extend your contacts*: there can be a feeling of anticlimax after a particularly good workshop or discussion session, or when a day school or residential study school is over. This can increase your feeling of isolation, so make sure that you back up the work you have done during these events by emailing your fellow students in order to continue working on ideas you had or begin preparing a presentation together, for example. This will allow you to make the most of the initial session and help you to settle back into your regular study tasks more easily.

- *Network*: your network need not be confined to your fellow students. Your course website might also be used by students on similar courses, and your professional life might offer you contacts whose input could be valuable. At all stages of your course, remain open to the possibility of increasing your networking base. Then, when you are feeling particularly isolated, especially if you are facing a difficult assignment or research task, you will have a range of support to draw upon.
- *Vary your tasks*: it is funny how particular tasks make us feel more isolated, even if we are spending relatively little time on them. If you loathe silent reading and find any excuse to escape, a four-hour session of reading and note taking late at night will leave you feeling as if you are the only person in the world who is studying. If this is your problem, make sure that you vary the location of your tasks (reading during your lunch hour at work or in the kitchen at home in the early evening might make it more palatable) and create a positive work pattern within your personalised timetable, adding enough variety each week so that you have contact time with others alongside your more solitary tasks. If you are working on a vocational course, introducing your colleagues to your work through lunchtime seminars is a good way to bring even more people into contact with your studying life.

You find it difficult to work with your course contacts

Finding it difficult to work with your course contacts can be a common problem in the early stages of a course, as you get used to working with a new set of people and, perhaps, a new way of studying. Much of this initial awkwardness and uncertainty will resolve itself quite quickly, but if you still have difficulties as your course progresses, try these approaches:

- *Analyse your needs*: if you are able to be specific about your needs, you are far more likely to get a useful response. Rather than asking for general support ('I am finding this assignment difficult'), be precise about the cause of your problems, if you can ('I am not sure about how to plan this assignment effectively'; 'I am finding it difficult to work within the word count' and so on). It is not always possible to be this specific, but any attempt to narrow down the details of your problem will offer your contacts clues as to how they can help you.
- *Be persistent*: you might naturally shy away from making a nuisance of yourself, but course contacts will not always be working to the same timetable as you, so make your needs clear. When you ask for urgent help, suggest the time to which you are working, for example, by adding 'answer appreciated by Friday' to your email title. If you do not get a

response, try again: it is possible that your email was lost, or that the contact simply forgot about your query. It will never mean that the contact does not want to help you, so try not to feel hesitant about this.

- *Define the boundaries*: it is essential that you understand the boundaries of each of your course relationships as early as possible. If you get an irrelevant or narrow response to your question, you might consider whether you have asked the right person. Asking the course administrators about who is the best person to help with your query is the easiest way around the difficulty.
- *Vary your communication methods*: some contacts will prefer to communicate by email, some by telephone and some in person. These entrenched preferences are difficult to shift, so it is better to ask all your contacts directly how they like to communicate with their students. This will eradicate the problem before it arises.

Your discussion group seems to be a waste of time

Thinking that a discussion group is a waste of time is not a common problem, but it will make you feel isolated within your studying if it happens to you. Rather than abandoning the group, there is plenty you can do to resolve the problem:

- *Analyse your response*: unless you know why you are experiencing a difficulty, it can become intractable. Spend some time analysing why you are finding a group unproductive, perhaps talking it through with your family and friends. It might be that your problem is one of personalities (one member of the group is too opinionated and loud; everyone else seems to be so knowledgeable) or practicalities (you have difficulty getting to the group; you find the timing inconvenient), but whatever the underlying cause, there will be a solution to the problem.
- *Talk to your group leader*: this is the obvious place to start, and your group leader is unlikely to be surprised by your problem: he or she has probably noticed the difficulty already and is just waiting for you to come forward. This approach will often improve the situation without you having to do anything further: your group leader can now take action to ensure that you feel included, suggest another time for the group to meet or relocate you to another, more conveniently located group.
- *Take steps together to improve the situation*: once you have broached the subject with your group leader, make sure that you offer feedback about how the changes are working for you. This will allow the leader to take further action if necessary: he or she will have plenty more ideas about how to improve the situation if it remains problematic.

- *Remember that you might be able to change groups*: although this might sound like a drastic solution, your course provider and group leader will not see it as a problem. Distance and open learning students often change groups, assuming that there are several available, for all sorts of reasons, so there is no reason to feel any anxicty about this. However, this solution is only likely to succeed if you have worked through the steps suggested above, so that you can be sure that a change of group is what you need, rather than trying new approaches within your existing group.

You are not enjoying your course

This is difficult: you might not be enjoying your course for all sorts of reasons, not all of which will be covered here. However, there are basic steps that you can take to begin working towards a solution:

- *Eliminate potential sources of the problem*: by working through the problems discussed in this chapter, you will be able to eliminate or identify potential problems areas. It is surprising how far-reaching the effects of one problem can be. If you are having difficulty with just one assignment, you might begin to feel that the backlog of work is never-ending. If you find the course website difficult to navigate, your frustration can overshadow the aspects of your course that you would otherwise enjoy. Try not to underestimate the effect of single problems, but if you have eliminated all the problems discussed here, you will have to continue in search of the cause of your unhappiness with your course.
- *Analyse the remaining possibilities*: there are some obvious problem areas that have not been covered in detail here because they are so unique to each student's circumstances, and the solution will be different in each case. You will need to think about these now, by considering whether perhaps you are just too tired to cope with studying or a life change has unsettled your routine to the point where you can no longer study in the same way. Maybe you are having financial difficulties, so are anxious about the money you are spending on your course, or you feel that the course is just not what you had expected from the course literature. These problems are difficult to pin down, often because the symptoms are so far removed from the cause, but you can enlist the help of your supporters and ask their opinion: problems are often obvious to those closest to us, even though we cannot see them ourselves.
- *Consider taking a break*: sometimes the problem is no more than that you have had enough of studying for a while. This is not a sign of failure

or an indication that you should not be studying, it is simply a recognition of the fact that life changes for us all over time, and what was easy six months ago may now have become unexpectedly difficult. A well-planned break can transform your attitude towards your course, so do not rule it out as a possibility.

- *Never suffer in silence*: you have family and friends to support you, but remember that your course providers will also want to help. Much of the work of course providers is not concerned with those students who are happily sailing through the course, but with those who are encountering problems. Your course providers will be ready with creative solutions and will want to help you once you have talked to them about the situation.

This chapter might read like a catalogue of disasters waiting to hit you. In reality, you will work through your course without encountering, or even being aware of, most of these problems, but when difficulties arise you need to be ready to counter them: early action is always preferable to leaving the situation alone in the hope that it might resolve itself without any action from you. It might, but you will have wasted valuable time worrying about the problem and it will hinder your progress until it is resolved. You have invested time and money in your course, but this can seem irrelevant when you have had enough and just want to give up; talk to your course contacts before you reach crisis point. If there is a solution to your problem, they will know about it and be able to help you implement it. Once you have resolved the problem, you will be able to move forward in a positive frame of mind to the next challenge on your course, with a new awareness that you are able to face and then overcome problems as they arise.

Spot guide

The key points to remember from this chapter:

- identifying your problem is the most important stage in solving it
- minor problems can seem overwhelming if they are left unattended
- you might feel that your studying is out of control, but it is more likely that just one aspect of your course is causing you problems
- once you have solved a problem, your overall performance will improve
- never assume that a problem is your fault: it is more likely to be your circumstances or the format of your course that is hindering your progress
- be methodical in your approach to problems, working through each of the suggestions in this chapter for your specific difficulty
- never suffer in silence: your course provider will have seen your problem before and will help you to take practical steps to get back on track

9 What Comes Next?

Troubleshooting guide

Use this chapter for help if:

- you want to continue to study beyond your current course
- you are not sure how to choose between courses
- you want to know how far your new skills and qualification will get you
- you are considering taking a break between courses
- you have not yet analysed your transferable skills
- you want to use your course to advance your career
- you are looking for a new job
- you are facing an appraisal and want to highlight your course
- you are not sure where to start in seeking out professional advancement
- you want to approach the job market in the most productive way
- you are not sure how to market your skills to an employer
- you want to create an effective CV

▶ Continuing to study

Distance and open learning can become addictive: no sooner have you finished a course than you decide that you have found the perfect course to move on to next. This is sometimes because your career development encourages you to keep studying; more often it is the case that distance and open learners enjoy a course and develop a pattern of studying that fits into their lifestyle and want to keep going. If this has happened to you, there is a temptation to move on to the next course in a rather haphazard way, but you can make the best use of your options if you take the time now to manage the process of moving from one course to another.

Considering your options

A return to the early chapters of this book is one way to ensure that you are covering all the options and assessing your next course as thoroughly as possible; but at this stage your focus will not just be on the course but also on you. Which parts of your course have you enjoyed most? Were there some aspects that you would be happy to avoid next time? Are there skills areas that you would particularly like to work on within the next stage of studying? Do you want a complete change in direction, or are you looking for a course that will allow you to study similar topics? Is there an independent area of research that you would like to develop in your next course? What does your mentor advise in terms of the way that your profession as a whole is developing? Has your tutor suggested a course to you? Have your circumstances changed during your current course, making one type of distance and open learning better than another?

When you were choosing your current course, you may have been making the decision alone, working through the options without always having a clear idea of what was involved. Your search was outward-looking as you considered different courses; now your search is also inward-looking as you think about your personal and intellectual development and your needs for the future. You are now in an excellent position to make an informed choice about where to go next.

Taking an overview of your position

Whilst you are gathering advice from your tutor, mentor and course providers (not forgetting that their Careers Advisory Service will also be able to help you), you can usefully make a set of notes on your current position. This will involve carrying out a skills audit similar to the one you produced at the outset of your course. You could also produce a written assessment of your studying experience, including in it those aspects that went well and those that were too burdensome, so that you develop a profile of the ideal course for you. Once you have done this, you could produce a course development sheet, on which you can map out the courses that you could complete in the next few years and how these might work together to advance your academic or professional position. In this way, you can take a long-term view of the benefits you can expect from continuing to study, either as a distance and open learner or, in the future, as an on-site student. You can work out which courses will gain you access to more advanced courses in the future and which will fit your requirements.

As you can see, this is going to require some thought and you will need to discuss your situation with your course contacts. It will also involve talking through your options with your family, friends and work colleagues. This will take time, so starting the process early is important. Although it may seem overzealous to begin to think about your next course so early, this process works best if you can leave yourself several weeks to work through your options in this way and several more weeks to find out about and apply for the next course.

Deciding between courses

In some ways you are in the best position to choose your next course: you have experience of distance and open learning and you will have heard about other courses. In other ways, you are in a risky position: you have enjoyed your course and might be tempted to move on to another course with little preparation so that you can continue to study. The way to avoid this risk is to undertake the preparatory work *before* you begin to look in detail at your specific course options. If you have a theoretical, ideal course profile, you can then safely look towards other courses, knowing that your study parameters are in place and you have a 'wish list' ready so that you can see how each course option will fit your studying, career and personal needs. Once you have done this, you can begin to use your network and supporters to best effect.

If you simply ask your fellow students in your discussion or workshop group or via your email network about which course they would recommend, you are likely to hear about other courses which would suit them, but which might not fulfil all your requirements. Instead, share your ideal course profile with them, so that they have a clear idea of the details of the course you are looking for, and then follow up each recommendation with thorough research. You will be able to dismiss some courses quickly and then return to your network with your final few options, so that they can share with you anything they have heard about the courses and suggest ways in which they might fit into your overall plan.

Considering your options with family and friends requires a similar approach. It is clearly important to involve these supporters in the process, but a set of vague questions will get you the most general of answers. Instead, work with them on your initial preparation, such as your skills audit and ideal course profile, then wait until you have several firm course options in front of you before you return to them for further help. It is essential that you listen to everything they have to say. Some of their points will be irrelevant, as they may not have undertaken distance and open learning themselves and so will not fully appreciate all that is involved, but some of what they have to say might be a revelation to you. You may have enjoyed your residential study schools, your family may have loathed them. You may have forgotten how stressed you felt over research assignments that they remember only too clearly. You might feel that the cost of a particular course is worthwhile; they might have difficulty seeing its relevance to your plans. By talking through the options in this structured, yet open way, you will eliminate problems that might otherwise cause you serious difficulties in the future, and you can also be sure that the course you choose is right for you and your family.

Using your qualification

As you consider your next course, remember that you will soon have a new qualification to offer. This seems obvious, but it is easy to reject the possibility of a course that appeals to you just because you do not have exactly the right qualification match according to the course literature. If you find a course that you would like to pursue, it is always a good idea to discuss your situation with the course providers, explaining what you have already done and considering with them how your recently acquired expertise might be of benefit to you on their course. You can put them in touch with your existing course provider so that they can talk through the details of your qualification and work out whether the course might be suitable for your needs and experience.

A similar principle applies when you are considering your long-term plans. As you approach each new course possibility, try to assess how it might fit into the long-term plans that you have made, how it might gain you access to far more advanced courses in the future and how you might be able to bring your existing knowledge and study skills to bear on this new challenge. You will also want to revisit the possibility of funding for your next course. Your employer and academic funding bodies might not have been able to support you financially on your last course, but your new qualification might make you eligible for financial help in the next course, so do not overlook this possibility.

Dovetailing courses

However widely your old and new courses diverge, you will still be able to analyse the work you have done so far and assess how it might help in your next course. For example, you might have material that was only indirectly related to your last course which you can now plan to reuse more effectively in your next course. Perhaps some sections of your tutor pack could be useful to you; downloading and printing off useful sections of your online course material is also a good idea before you move on. At the very least you will have some relevant study skills notes that you made during your course and a research notebook that still has outstanding queries in it. This material should not be abandoned but be kept at the ready as you approach a new course.

It can be helpful to overhaul your filing system as you move from one course to the next. Work through your various files, remove any material that you think might be useful to you in the next course and file it separately. These will be your 'base files', similar in a way to the files you created with your tutor material at the outset of your course. They may never be used in their entirety, but you will have material that will translate from one course to another and, when the pressure is on as your next course progresses, you can access this material relatively easily. These files serve several purposes. They will keep your existing study material in order, provide reassurance that you are not starting again entirely from scratch and arranging them will give you something constructive to do once your course has ended. This is important because you can be unexpectedly visited with a feeling of anticlimax in the time between courses, but taking positive steps such as this towards preparing for your next course can help to overcome this feeling.

Assessing your skills development

When you carried out your skills audit at the outset of your course, it might have been a rather muddled process, with you struggling to see the relevance of your past experiences to the new challenge that lay ahead of you. Now, you have a great advantage. You have already begun to develop your skills base and you will have seen the relevance of approaching this in a methodical way as your course progresses. I have already suggested that you consider one or two obvious skills areas that you want to develop as part of the process of choosing your next course; you can also use the time between courses to manage this process in more detail. When you have time, and particularly if you are feeling at a bit of a loss once the studying is over, work back through your personalised timetables and skills development plans and see how far you have come. This is a positive experience in itself, but it will also allow you to focus on where to go next. You can produce a new set of skills development sheets and complete the first few sections, assessing your skills base in each area as it now stands and identifying activities within your next course that you believe might help you to develop these areas further. Things may not work out exactly as you expect, but you will have your skills development plans in place before you start the course, which will take some pressure off you as you tackle your initial workload.

Taking a break

I have already mentioned the feeling of anticlimax that can come with the completion of a course. The anticipation of this feeling can lead distance and open learning students to move straight from one course into another, without ever considering a break in their studying. This might be the right thing to do, but it is worth at least thinking about taking a break from studying for a while between courses. When you come to analyse the situation, you might find that what you will miss, at least in the first few weeks after a course is complete, is not so much the studying as the structure and purpose that it gave to your weekly routine. If this is the case, but you feel that a break from the studying itself might be helpful in allowing you to rest for a while, you could usefully produce a personalised timetable for the period between courses. This will not be the same as your normal personalised timetable, as it will include predominantly work and home life activities, but it will ensure that you do not lose all sense of structure and will help you to focus on what is important in the time that you have away from studying. If you are changing direction, know that you have plenty of preparation to do for your next course or just feel that you will miss studying, you could include some study-related tasks in the personalised timetable, as long as you recognise that this is supposed to be a break and give yourself the chance to have some completely free time away from your studying.

The advantage of producing a personalised timetable in these circumstances is that it allows you to approach your next course in a methodical way, just as I suggested you return to studying if you take a break during a course: all the same principles will apply. Timing here is going to be crucial. You will not want to feel as if you have had no break at all, but you will also want to avoid feeling as if you are beginning your new course with too little mental and emotional preparation. As with so many other aspects of managing your distance and open learning career, getting the balance right is the answer to the problem, and a personalised timetable in these circumstances can ensure that you are achieving this.

Advancing your career

If the course you are completing is part of your career development structure, you will need now to assess how you can put it to use. Even if your course was never intended to be a stepping stone to career advancement, you do now have more to offer a potential employer and you might find yourself reconsidering your career options. This might not entail changing your job; it is equally useful to assess what you have to offer in preparation for your next promotion opportunity or annual appraisal. The hurdle you might face is that your current employer, and any potential new employer, might not fully understand the details of your course. If your course is directly relevant to your career, this will not be problem as long as you can produce a CV or internal résumé for appraisal which accurately reflects the nature and content of your course: this will be covered in detail later in this chapter. If your course is not directly related to your career, it will still give you a significant advantage within your career development, as long as you can package yourself in the most effective way, in terms of the experience you have gained and the skills you have acquired.

Assessing your transferable, marketable skills

Having suggested that your newly expanded skills base is an important tool in your career development, it is worth considering how you can most effectively market this to employers. You already have a skills inventory that is relevant to you: now you must make it attractive to employers. There are four stages to this process.

Update your skills inventory

Before you market yourself, it is helpful to update your skills inventory without any reference to a specific job. Simply work through your skills development sheets and list your skills as you did with your initial skills audit, grading them as before, but this time also producing evidence to show how you have used and developed these skills. It is important to be honest with yourself. If you know that you still have some way to go with some skills areas, it is better to make a note of this now rather than ignoring it. It will not necessarily be a disadvantage; it might help to focus your job search as you either avoid jobs that are too demanding in that area, or choose jobs because they offer you the chance for further development. At this stage your skills audit will be more extensive than the example below, but it will look something like this.

Skill	Rating	Example
Working to deadlines	HIGH	• Produced extended research project on time • Prepared for each residential study school • Returned assessed essays to deadline • Maintained personalised timetable

(continued)

Giving presentations	HIGH	• Led discussion groups with a presentation each time • Gave group presentation on work-based project • Delivered a conference paper
Teamwork	MEDIUM	• Developed email network and maintained contact throughout course • Organised workshop session for other students
Report writing	HIGH	• Produced assessed report assignments, gaining good grades • Quarterly reports to employer on CPD within course • Work-based project report used within employer's training scheme seminars

Remember that you are likely to be too modest about your achievements and may be underestimating your skills base. In the example above the student has rated his teamwork ability as 'medium', because in his view he has been working in relative isolation for much of his course. An employer might see this differently, focusing on the fact that he maintained an active and productive email network support system throughout his course and worked well within several different workshop groups; if he can do that, he is a natural team player. The way to avoid being falsely modest is to enlist the help of family, friends and work colleagues. Prepare your skills audit as in the example above by yourself, with no input from others. Then ask your supporters to look it over with you and suggest further examples that you might use at interview or on your CV to demonstrate your skills. The likelihood is that your supporters will want to upgrade every skills area to 'high', but you will be able to work through the sheet again, differentiating between those skills you are convinced do rate highly and those you still believe should be rated lower. A potential employee who claims to be strong in every skill area is unlikely to be convincing at interview; an employer will feel more positive towards a candidate who has examined his or her skill set, is sure about certain areas of excellence, recognises a need to improve in other areas and is keen to do so.

Identify the key tasks in your current or potential job

When you have a skills sheet such as the one above in place, you can begin to assess the skills required in the job for which you are applying, or the skills that your employer would like you to develop as part of your continuing professional development. Remember that you are looking here at skills, not tasks. It is only by identifying the skills involved in succeeding in each task that you can fully relate your distance and open learning skills base to your professional skills base. Your professional skills requirement sheet (matched here to the skills audit above) will look something like this.

Task	**Skill**
Increasing sales figures by 25 per cent within next quarter	Working to deadlines (high skill level)
Chairing quarterly sales meetings	Giving presentations (high skill level)
Motivating sales team	Teamwork (medium skill level)
Producing monthly sales report	Report writing (high skill level)

Collect evidence
Collecting evidence is relatively easy, but do not fall into the trap of becoming too generalised. You have already identified the skills required and know that they match your own, but at this stage you must be able to offer specific examples to prove your skills development, choosing the most relevant example in each case. This might be the example you feel is the most impressive or one you would like to talk about at interview. Your skills match sheet will look something like this.

Task	**Skill**	**Evidence**
Increasing sales figures by 25 per cent within next quarter	Working to deadlines (high skill level)	Produced extended research project on time
Chairing quarterly sales meetings	Giving presentations (high skill level)	Delivered a conference paper
Motivating sales team	Teamwork (medium skill level)	Organised workshop session for other students

(continued)

Producing monthly sales report	Report writing (high skill level)	Work-based project report used within employer's training scheme seminars

Show how your personal qualities will be of benefit

It would be so easy if employers were just looking for the right skills set before offering you a job. In reality, this is not the case. They are looking for the right person, someone who can fit in with their team and whose skills can be used to the full because of the personal qualities they are bringing to the tasks in hand. Any distance and open learning student could claim to be able to work to deadlines and, in the absence of any evidence to the contrary, the employer would be forced to take this at face value. What you need to do is prove that you did work to deadlines, using the examples you already have in place, and then show that understanding the personal qualities you possess enabled you to become so efficient. You must bring together the information from the sheets you have produced so far if you are to demonstrate this to an employer. Your final 'sales sheet' will now look something like this.

Task	**Skill**	**Evidence**	**Personal qualities**
Increasing sales figures by 25 per cent within next quarter	Working to deadlines (high skill level)	Produced extended research project on time	Determined Organised Motivated
Chairing quarterly sales meetings	Giving presentations (high skill level)	Delivered a conference paper	Confident Well-prepared communicator
Motivating sales team	Teamwork (medium skill level)	Organised workshop session for other students	Enthusiastic Approachable Committed
Producing monthly sales report	Report writing (high skill level)	Work-based project report used within employer's training scheme seminars	Perfectionist Disciplined Professional Analytical

You will by now have worked through a lengthy process of assessment and analysis in order to produce a sales sheet that accurately reflects your personality and developing skills base and is attractive to an employer who is looking for a certain type of person with a well-defined skills set. You are now ready to move ahead, by either impressing your employer at your next appraisal (and perhaps gaining financial support for your next course) or selling your skills to potential employers.

Selling yourself in the job market

It is an often publicised fact that the vast majority of vacancies are not advertised: the figure is sometimes put as high as 80 per cent. This leaves you with a dilemma: you know that the jobs are out there somewhere, you are keen to make the most of your new qualification and skills but you are not sure exactly which job you want or how to get it. The first thing to do is to carry out some research. You might already have some options in place from your networking, and your course may have been designed to prepare its students for a particular career area. Even if this is the case, carry out some careers research and think as widely as you can before committing yourself. Your course provider's Careers Advisory Service is not just for full-time students: they will be able to work through the possibilities with you, perhaps offering you online personality and aptitude tests to help you to narrow down the options. You may have already found that an online career development module was part of your distance and open learning course structure.

Before you take the next step, there are some vital points to remember: you have just successfully completed a demanding course, you probably have a new qualification and you will be a valuable asset to any organisation. Never sell yourself short; you may have to compromise on some aspects of your employment, we all do, but do not allow yourself to be persuaded that you have to continue at the same level of employment despite the fact that you feel ready for a new challenge. Now is the time to capitalise on all your hard work: be clear about what you have to offer and remain resolute in getting what you want.

Once you have decided on an area or more probably several areas that interest you, you are still left with the problem of succeeding in the job market. There are several ways in which you can tackle this, and using a combination of all these approaches will give you the best chance of success.

Careers fairs

Your course providers may run careers fairs for their students; if they are a university- or college-wide event they can be crowded out by eager undergraduates, but this does not prevent you from taking a look at what is on offer: distance and open learning students will be as welcome as any other students. Remember that you are making judgements about the organisations at the fair as well as allowing them to assess you as a potential employee. Make sure that you gather as much information as you can in this relatively informal setting, but keep an eye on the people who are there to represent each organisation. If they seem negative, rather too pushy for your liking or, as can sometimes happen, they just look downright miserable, see this as a possible reflection of the organisation for whom they are working.

Your course provider

The amount of involvement that course providers have with career development varies from course to course, but it is worth finding out if there are ways in which they can help you. Course providers sometimes hold detailed information about the career development of their past students, as this helps them in their recruitment of new students, which can be an easy way of beginning your research. It may be possible for you to make contact directly with distance and open learners who have successfully entered a career area in which you have an interest. As with so much else, your course secretary will be able to point you in the right direction.

Newspapers and journals

Newspapers and journals are an obvious place to begin, but be as creative as you can in your searching and remember that whilst organisations might be specific about their requirements in terms of qualifications or the 'standard' candidate they expect to apply for a job, you now have your sales sheet in place, ready to explain why they should be offering you an interview. If you notice that a particular organisation is placing several adverts for different positions, you can be reasonably sure that it is running a recruitment drive and it will be worthwhile contacting it in case it is planning to extend its recruitment to an area that interests you. Specialist journals in your field will carry advertisements for vacancies, but again, do not just take the initial information at face value: if an organisation looks interesting, give it a call.

The internet

The internet is an increasingly accessible and popular source of information about careers and job vacancies, one to which you will turn early in your search. Your experience as a distance and open learner will help you here: you are already used to using the internet as an everyday part of your studying life. As with your studying tasks, make sure that you are targeted in your approach, or you might waste hours looking at sites that are only marginally useful, or simply logging on to sites that are run by job agencies when a direct approach to employers might be more productive. If you find an organisation that interests you, use the internet to find out as much as you can about it and then make contact directly.

Job agencies

There are many useful job agencies, but many more will be useless to you, because they do not specialise in your field of interest or they are overloaded with candidates and short of vacancies to offer them. Be selective: find out which are the best agencies to contact and then take control of the situation. If they want to produce a CV for you, make sure that you have the final say on its content and presentation: they will not understand the detail of your distance and open learning course as well as you do, and you have already put in the necessary work to highlight the skills and personal qualities that you feel are relevant. If they want to send you for an interview, make absolutely certain that you know where they are sending you and make sure that the job is at a level that reflects your current status rather than just your previous career experience.

Networking

You already have your most influential and important network in place: your course contacts and fellow students. In the final stages of your course (preferably at least six weeks prior to completion), identify those contacts who will be most useful: fellow students who are also looking for work in a similar area, professional contacts who already work in the area and your tutor, supervisor and professional mentor. It makes sense to create a mail group that includes all these people, so that you can all circulate information easily. This might be details of opportunities with organisations in your area, addresses for websites that might be of interest or news of careers events that some of you could attend. Online networks such as these can extend over many years, as each member continues to progress within a similar career area.

Direct contact

Direct contact is the most challenging, but also the most effective way to get into a career, particularly for distance and open learning students who may not simply be applying for specific jobs, but might also be in the process of finding out about general career opportunities in their new area of expertise. By contacting organisations directly, you will be getting behind the advertised job market into what is often referred to as the 'hidden' job market, where job vacancies are filled by word of mouth rather than a formal recruitment procedure. You might be making 'warm calls', that is, contacting an employer who came to speak at a residential study school or who you met as a result of a career or research placement, or 'cold calls', where you will be approaching an organisation without any knowledge of whether it is recruiting or not. Making direct contact is an efficient use of your time and will be necessary even if you are responding to an advert: in this case, you will need to know whether the vacancy still exists (this can save you hours of wasted time), whether you can fill their requirements and whether the organisation is one that suits you. There are techniques to this approach that you will need to master:

- Do the research: if you have heard of an organisation that interests you, find out as much as you can about it, perhaps through a website, by getting hold of a company brochure or using your online network.
- Prepare your paperwork in advance: before you telephone, have your CV and sales sheet in front of you, with a list of questions you want to ask, and a pen and paper ready to take notes. Be ready for your enquiry to turn into an informal telephone interview. If you realise that there are new questions you can ask in future calls, add them to your list as you go along. You will probably find that, by the end of the first three calls, your 'script' is twice as long as it was at the outset.
- Have a series of telephone calls arranged before you begin: make a list of a dozen organisations that appeal to you and then brace yourself to make all the calls in one day.
- Do not be disappointed if you cannot get through to the human resources department on your first try: receptionists can be an invaluable source of information that is not readily available elsewhere, so keep them talking about the organisation if you can. You can always call back later if you cannot get through to the right department on your first attempt.
- Begin with your least favoured option and work up. You might find that on your first call your mouth goes dry and you forget what you wanted to say. It will not matter if this call is a disaster: you have plenty more options in front of you. You will be amazed at how quickly you become adept at this exercise.
- If you suspect that the first call is going to be a nightmare, when you might forget what you wanted to say or just dry up altogether, dial 141

(so that your number cannot be traced) before you make the call and, if it all goes wrong, just put the telephone down. They will never know who was calling them and you can try again later when you become more expert.

- Be ready to enjoy yourself. Although this exercise can be terrifying in prospect, comfort yourself with the fact that it is probably the best way to get a job and discover how far your distance and open learning course will get you in the careers market, and you will find that, with practice, it can be a satisfying and enjoyable process.
- Avoid the temptation to be negative. If an organisation has no vacancies at the moment, this does not mean that it will not have any jobs on offer next week. If you can get a conversation going and arrange to send your CV, it can get back to you when an opportunity arises: this really does happen. It is expensive for an organisation to recruit new staff: if your details are on file it is more cost-effective for it to come back directly to you when a vacancy arises. If you want to make yourself even more visible and it seems appropriate, ask to visit its premises so as to learn more about how it operates. This will give you the chance to have an informal chat in advance of any positions becoming vacant.
- See this as a fact finding mission. This exercise is as much about you exploring what the organisation has to offer as it is about it assessing you. If the receptionist is rude and the manager is unhelpful and unsure about what it might have on offer, you might decide that you are not interested in it, which will save you the trouble of applying to that organisation when it does advertise vacancies.

You have two challenges ahead as you target your new career. You are trying to find out exactly where you want to be in the future and researching all the possible leads, but you are doing all this whilst still trying to get used to the 'new you', the successful distance and open learning student with an up-to-date knowledge base and impressive skills set who has so much to offer an employer. By targeting the career market directly, doing your research and making the telephone calls, you will be tackling both these areas. As you carry out your career research, you will get a better idea of where to go and as you call organisations, you will feel increasingly confirmed in your new status.

Producing a CV

Achieving your career goals will involve creating an impressive CV, one that both reflects your professional experience and highlights your distance and open learning course. You will need to be organised from the outset. Keep a file on each organisation you have approached, so that you can refer back to the notes you made during the telephone call, a copy of the application form you filled in and the CV you sent. Keeping your records up to date need not be a chore: in reality, you will find it reassuring as it imposes some structure on the process and is not dissimilar to the way you have already approached the management of your distance and open learning course. When you become anxious about your chances of getting a job, you can look into your files and remind yourself that you are doing everything you can do towards that end, which is a comfort if things seem to be moving too slowly.

When you succeed in a telephone call, you will probably be asked to send your CV to the organisation. In some cases, successful candidates are asked to complete an application form only after they have been interviewed, just to satisfy the protocol of the organisation concerned. Your CV is going to be vital to you.

Before you can begin to write your CV, you need to take a step back and consider what you want it to do for you. You are trying to sell yourself to an employer, and, like any successful marketing strategy, you need to know as much as you can about the sales situation before you begin. There are three main points to bear in mind:

- *Know who you are*: that is, know who you are from the point of view of employment. What are you selling? What are your unique selling points? You already have a sales sheet in place, so this is merely a case of reminding yourself of your skills and personal qualities and deciding which of these to highlight on each targeted CV you produce. Once you have completed your CV, pin it up somewhere where you can see it every day. This will boost your confidence and remind you of the professional image you are projecting.
- *Know where you want to be*: even if you are applying for a vacancy that has been advertised, you will not have enough information from an advert to make the best sales pitch. You will need to make a telephone call to find out more about the vacancy and the organisation. You will need to know not just about the job on offer, but also about how the working methods and ethos of the organisation will fit into any future plans you have to undertake further distance and open learning courses.
- *Know what they want*: you can usually get hold of a copy of a full job description and person specification if you contact the organisation, and this will give you essential clues about how to target your CV and

application form. If you check the website or get a copy of the company brochure or marketing material, you can learn about the culture of the organisation and so work out what sort of person it is likely to employ. You course contacts may also be able to offer you some inside information about how the company works and, possibly, whether it might support you in future distance and open learning courses, either financially or practically within your new job.

At every stage in this process of learning about your prospective employer, remember that you are free to pull out. You have not yet even begun to write your CV or fill out an application form, so if your instinct is telling you that this is not the right company for you, trust to it and move on to your next prospect.

If the organisation is still one to which you want to apply once you have done this research, you will begin to prepare your CV. Remember that your CV is your sales pitch, so you have to make each word count. One of the first decisions that you will make is how to represent your distance and open learning course. You will be using your experience as evidence of your suitability for the job throughout the CV, but if you are considering a change in career direction as a result of your course, you might choose to highlight your course above your career history so that the potential employer cannot miss its relevance and value. Although you will work within the most effective format for you, the CV outlined below uses a format that works well. I have taken for this example our student from earlier chapters. She has now successfully completed her diploma in human resources and is applying for a job as a training and HR development manager.

Curriculum Vitae

Rachel Weston
43 Asters Road, BRISTOL BS3 4TG
Tel: 0162 634 8201; mobile: 07660 953 2728
email: r.weston@aol.com

A committed professional with experience in human resources and training. An excellent communicator and team player who combines recent, up-to-date qualifications with a creative and enthusiastic approach to new challenges.

RELEVANT SKILLS AND EXPERIENCE

Human resources development: During my recent diploma course I undertook an extensive work-based project on recruitment and retention amongst graduates.

Training: I have been involved in training at many levels, from mentoring new staff within my current post to leading study workshops for up to 20 students, where my enthusiasm and organisational skills were essential.

Communication: I have experience of dealing with clients and colleagues by telephone, in writing and in person. I am particularly adept at developing and maintaining online networks.

Teamwork: I have worked as a member of several successful teams giving group presentations, arranging conferences and undertaking research projects.

Organisation: I am a highly organised individual and this was vital to the successful completion my distance and open learning course, in which I completed each assignment on time and to the specified requirements.

Information technology: I have undertaken courses in Office 2000, Front Page and PowerPoint. I am keen to continue to develop my IT skills in the workplace.

EDUCATION

2002–04: Diploma in Human Resources, specialising in the impact of training upon the recruitment and retention of graduate staff. During the course I was involved in:

- Carrying out a major research project into the development of training techniques within the workplace.
- Undertaking a work-based project covering the recruitment and retention of diverse groups of staff.
- Giving several professional-level presentations, both individually and as part of a group.
- Working online and in my own time, necessitating a high level of self-discipline and motivation. I was able to complete the course on time and gained a distinction for my research project.

1987–93: Honours Degree (2:1) (part time) in Psychology, with modules also successfully completed in Politics and Sociology. My dissertation, entitled 'Managing Stress in the Modern Workplace', formed an important part of my course.

1982–84: A levels gained in English (B), Sociology (C) and Law (E)
GCE O levels gained in ten subjects, including English, Mathematics, ICT, French and German

(continued)

PROFESSIONAL DEVELOPMENT

Successful completion in 1997 of course to develop training techniques.

Three-year part-time counselling course completed in 1995.

Courses recently undertaken in Office 2000, Front Page and PowerPoint. I have a working knowledge of a variety of design packages and some experience of accounting software.

I have recently attended a series of conferences organised by the IPD; I have also given a paper entitled 'The value of counselling methods within human resources.'

CAREER HISTORY

1994–present: Human resources administrator (assistant to human resources director) for Deltina Limited, Bristol, a manufacturing organisation with 200 staff. My responsibilities have included:

- recruitment of new staff; initial interviews
- mentoring graduate recruits and administering their training programme
- organising annual induction sessions
- arranging staff appraisal sessions
- managing the day-to-day running of the human resources office
- sitting in on a board-level recruitment committee

1985–92: Salary administration clerk with Teftone Limited, Sheffield, responsible for the salary administration for a workforce of 30.

ADDITIONAL INFORMATION

I am a member of the Institute for Professional Development.
I hold a first aid certificate.
I hold a certificate in counselling and am a member of the British Counselling Association.
I am physically fit and have a current driving licence.
My interests include amateur dramatics, reading and music.

References are available on request

As you can see, this student has made the most of both her experience and her distance and open learning course, whilst playing down the chronological gaps in her education and employment. This is the CV of a highly dynamic and hard-working distance and open learning student, whose course is directly relevant to her career path. Having produced a sales sheet in line with the requirements of the vacancy, she is able to highlight those skills and personal qualities that make her well suited to the post, and she will be able to discuss her experience in a succinct and relevant way at interview. Your CV will not identically follow this one, but this example shows how your course can be integrated into your overall selling strategy.

For the vast majority of distance and open learning students, the successful completion of their course is about more than just gaining a qualification. It is about developing as a person, emerging from the course with a wider knowledge base and a newly acquired sense of fulfilling a long-held ambition. As this period of study comes to an end, you have proved that you can successfully manage a distance and open learning course, and in doing this you have overcome the hurdles in your way, developed your skills and sharpened your focus on your goals. You are an adept communicator, a self-disciplined learner and a highly motivated student. You are now ready to represent yourself to the world as a newly qualified expert in your field, confident about your skills and ready to move towards the next challenge. Good luck!

Spot guide

The key points to remember from this chapter:

- the move from your current course to the next course should be approached in a methodical way, using your experience of distance and open learning
- take an overview of your position to assess where you need to go next
- enlist the help of family, friends and work colleagues as you choose between courses
- avoid the temptation to abandon the material you have already accumulated: use it to dovetail your current and your next course
- if you are intending to take a break between courses, use the advice in this chapter to make it as productive a time as possible
- you have an impressive and developing skills base: analyse it now as you consider new courses or your career advancement
- you have developed marketable skills within your course: any potential employer needs to be shown this
- your personal qualities are as important as your skills: remember to include them within your CV
- be creative and persistent about finding the perfect job for your new status and experience
- always produce a targeted CV, one that reflects the skills, experience and personal qualities that your target company is seeking: do the research
- you will succeed, whether you are looking for a new job, reassessing your current position or moving on to the next course: all it takes is determination, evaluation and belief in yourself

Recommended Reading

Clarke, A. *e-Learning Skills* (Basingstoke: Palgrave Macmillan, 2004)

Coombes, H. *Research Using IT* (Basingstoke: Palgrave – now Palgrave Macmillan, 2001)

Cottrell, S. *Skills for Success: The Personal Development Planning Handbook* (Basingstoke: Palgrave Macmillan, 2003)

Cottrell, S. *The Study Skills Handbook, 2nd edn* (Basingstoke: Palgrave Macmillan, 2003)

Fanthome, C. *Work Placements – A Survival Guide for Students* (Basingstoke: Plagrave Macmillan, 2004)

Greetham, B. *How to Write Better Essays* (Basingstoke: Palgrave – now Palgrave Macmillan, 2001)

Lewis, M. and Reinders, H. *Study Skills for Speakers of English as a Second Language* (Basingstoke: Palgrave Macmillan, 2003)

Littleford, D. Halstead, J. and Mulraine, C. *Career Skills: Opening Doors into the Job Market* (Basingstoke: Palgrave Macmillan, 2004)

Peck, J. and Coyle, M. *The Student's Guide to Writing* (Basingstoke: Macmillan – now Palgrave Macmillan, 1999)

Rose, J. *The Mature Student's Guide to Writing* (Basingstoke: Palgrave – now Palgrave Macmillan, 2001)

van Emden, J. and Becker, L. *Presentation Skills for Students* (Basingstoke: Palgrave Macmillan, 2004)

Index